BILLION DOLLAR MIND

Practical Guide for Mental Strength
In the Game of Life

Rick Macci and Dr. Niva
(Nivedita Uberoi Jerath MD, MS)

BILLION-DOLLAR MIND

Copyright © 2023 by Nivedita (Niva) Uberoi Jerath MD, MS and Rick Macci

All rights reserved. No part of this book may be reproduced or used without the publisher's express written consent, except for brief quotations used in a book review.

This book doesn't replace expert medical advice or consultation.

DEDICATION

Rick Macci: This book is dedicated to the world. Even though I have been fortunate to be on a tennis court my whole life, I have not just changed strokes, but have also changed lives. In fact, I'm more of a life coach than a tennis coach. Everyone needs a mentor, everyone needs a pat on the back, and everyone needs motivation. I've been wired with those unreal Midwest values growing up in Greenville, Ohio and treating others even better than I treat myself. With this book, I want to share it with the world, because I really feel that's always been my calling and if the reader can even change **ONE** mindset, we all have won **WON.**

Dr. Niva (Nivedita Jerath): This book is dedicated to my parents and my remarkable daughters, Athma and Ziva, exemplars of intelligence and beauty. To my mother, Veena Uberoi Jerath, who initiated my journey into mental resilience at a tender age. While she adjusted my tennis technique at the age of 11, her guidance instilled within me the importance of nurturing mental strength. Mom's wisdom about "cultivating a robust mind to navigate criticism, feedback, and the pressures of attaining greatness" sparked my fervor to develop mental fortitude. This trait transcended tennis, permeating all facets of my life. To my father, Mohan Jerath, who adorned our home with books penned by Norman Vincent Peale. I vividly recall his words from my early years when, at the age of seven, he imparted that our attitude remains within our control, an anchor irrespective of circumstances. He would assert, "Our attitude, not our aptitude, dictates our altitude." To my daughters, Athma and Ziva, and to every child across the globe: My aspiration is for you to employ this book as a tool to construct an unshakeable mind, a sanctuary impervious to disturbances, allowing you to triumph regardless of external tumult. To Athma and Ziva's father, Chandan Reddy, who supplied the house with his endless love of excellent books. To Chandan's parents, Gopal and Kala Reddy for their unwavering support of Athma and nursing her back to health.

TABLE OF CONTENTS

PREFACE	1
AUTHOR INTRODUCTION	5
CHAPTER 1: The Importance of Our Thoughts	9
CHAPTER 2: Neuroanatomy Behind Thought Control	25
CHAPTER 3: Thinking Loops are Traps	41
CHAPTER 4: Sensory Mental Diet and Exercise: Positive Thoughts	53
CHAPTER 5: Sensory Mental Diet and Exercise: Positive Associations	65
CHAPTER 6: Sensory Mental Diet and Exercise: Visualization	77
CHAPTER 7: Sensory Mental Diet and Exercise: Self-love	87
CHAPTER 8: Motor Mental Diet and Exercise: Positive Affirmations	95
CHAPTER 9: Motor Mental Diet and Exercise: Letting Go of Past Memories	107
CHAPTER 10: Motor Mental Diet and Exercise: Flip it fast!	117
CHAPTER 11: Motor Mental Diet and Exercise: Humor to Improve Mental Health and Relaxation	127
CHAPTER 12: Motor Mental Diet and Exercise: Positive Attitude	137
CHAPTER 13: Motor Mental Diet and Exercise: Gratitude	147
CHAPTER 14: Motor Mental Diet and Exercise: Self-Confidence	155
CHAPTER 15: Motor Mental Diet and Exercise: Self-Discipline	165
CHAPTER 16: Motor Mental Diet and Exercise: Self-Improvement	177
CHAPTER 17: Motor Mental Diet and Exercise: Focus	191
CHAPTER 18: Motor Mental Diet and Exercise: Self-Motivation	201
CONCLUSION	213
ABOUT THE AUTHORS	221
REFERENCES	225

PREFACE

Under the scorching sun of an Orlando, Florida bike ride, a day unfurled that would leave an indelible mark on my life. As I pedaled with unwavering determination, the heat bore down on me, but I channeled my frustration into the pavement, propelling myself forward. A victor in my professional realm, my mind was fortified, yet I found myself grappling with failure. Failure in relationships, failure in life's grand tapestry, and failure in my career's pursuit. Amidst a sick child, a fractured family, and a descending trajectory, there was only one direction left to go: up.

Strapping my cell phone to my bike, I embarked on a mission to dissect the roots of my shortcomings. I listened to conversations about the environment and the dialogue resonated as I navigated through the negativity surrounding me. Pausing to sift through the noise in my mind, I discerned the unproductive impact of this negativity. Continuing my quest for enlightenment, I absorbed insights, replaying a transformative discourse to shed unconstructive thoughts that reverberated within me. I braked and surveyed my surroundings, a revelation dawning upon me—the genesis of my failures lay within my own thoughts.

Cycles of past shattered relationships, the anguish, the tears, and the retreat of cherished ones, all became apparent as culprits. My academic prowess at esteemed institutions hadn't equipped me to fathom human intricacies; solitude had been my companion since childhood, a scholarly recluse. Shifting focus, I confronted the most piercing source of pain—a legacy of misunderstandings, eroded trust, the wake of severed ties, and the solitude that ensued. Those instances were beyond repair. The sky overhead beckoned, compelling me to release these tormenting thoughts, observing them ascend into the heavens like balloons. And there, amidst the azure expanse, I found solace.

A smile played on my lips as I endorsed a newfound clarity. Engaging in conversation with a couple, I sensed a departure from the repeated thoughts of agony. However, the evening bore a resurgence of tormenting thoughts, igniting anguish and tears. Obligations beckoned; work required peak performance, lest my career falter. Nightfall witnessed me awakening to a resonating realization to overcome my situation and paralyzing thoughts: surrounding myself with supportive colleagues, reflecting my positivity, hard work, and achievement. Galvanized, I leaped to my computer, immersing in a discourse on excellence and solitude. A realization crystallized—I was, in essence, entitled to solitude, no longer defying the norm.

A mirror unveiled my true identity—an individual untethered to trivial routines, ceaselessly harboring grand aspirations of altering the world, nurturing success, and fostering positivity. Self-acceptance emerged as paramount—my daily confidant embodied diligence, aspiration, intensity, and an unrelenting pursuit of excellence. My diet, exercise, and unwavering dedication bespoke my commitment. While my thoughts spiraled uncontrollably, centered around isolation and fractured bonds, I recognized the misalignment—I had unwittingly surrounded myself with a discordant crowd, rendering me painfully alone. Determined to reverse the trajectory, I resolved to cultivate a circle that resonated with my essence. That fateful night heralded transformation, altering my thought patterns irrevocably. Dawn unveiled a metamorphosed self, invigorated by an immediate realization that nothing should be holding me back, especially myself.

Gathering my musings, dreams, and acquired wisdom, I hastened to create social media digital channels—a canvas for my ideas. Amidst heartbreak's embrace, productivity burgeoned, and creativity blossomed. Revisiting my core essence, an initiative to aid others crystallized—an alliance with an eminent coach held the promise of impacting mental resilience and thought governance. Memories stirred of my own legendary tennis coach, Rick Macci, whose teachings on mental fortitude resonated profoundly. The decision to reconnect with him proved pivotal, infusing purpose into my existence. The culmination of years steeped in pain and endurance delivered this book, a testament to the evolution of thought mastery. Rick and I envision its resonance permeating the world, an offering to elevate minds universally.

AUTHOR INTRODUCTION

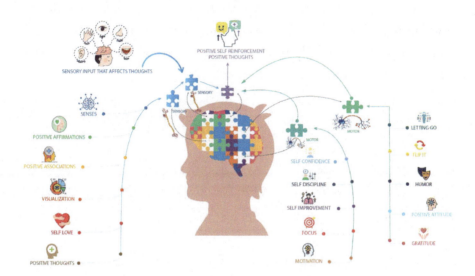

The chapters are the fundamental building blocks to develop a strong billion-dollar mind and each chapter reinforces and fits with the others, akin to building a puzzle. The mind is a stepping stone from failure to success. This book is intended for the world—for everyone desiring to improve their mental strength and seeking to elevate their level of achievement, happiness, and contentment in life. Make it a habit to revisit this book regularly to reinforce your mental fortitude and generate the thoughts essential for achieving your ambitions, thereby cultivating a mindset akin to a billion-dollar asset. The human mind holds the key to both success and failure in life. Mastering one's mind equates to mastering the world. This book aims to guide you in constructing a "billion-dollar mind" through our practical techniques. Its purpose is to forge a billion-dollar toolbox, fostering the development of an unyielding mind. We believe those who triumph over their minds can attain the value of a billion dollars, irrespective of monetary wealth. Conversely, possessing billions and not having control over one's mindset may still lead to a life mired in misery, discontent, and solitude.

Our minds are fundamentally flawed. Even though we know mental toughness and positivity are important, we can still lose our mental and thought control in the most emotional and heightened situations. This book will help build our mental toolbox to resist negative or destructive thoughts.

"Life is a game of inches and so is tennis, from one ear to another."

-RICK MACCI

CHAPTER 1

The Importance of Our Thoughts

Our minds exhibit imperfections. Why is it that our thoughts exhibit such frequent vacillation? How is it that a solitary raindrop can darken our day, while a burst of sunshine can instantly illuminate it? Why do we tend to focus on our weaknesses rather than our strengths? Why does unease grip us when someone remains unresponsive or fails to communicate with us? Why do our thoughts possess this capricious nature?

How often have we suffered due to the deficiencies of our minds—lapses in concentration, negative ideation, wandering thoughts, and even our own self-doubt? As our reliance on Artificial Intelligence and technology grows, our minds are the distinguishing factor. Nonetheless, despite their potency, human minds retain inherent flaws, characterized by their mercurial disposition and propensity for negativity. The power of a positive relationship cannot be underestimated, as it possesses the potential to shift one from the clutches of failure to the heights of triumph through its profound influence on our mindset. Our thinking processes are susceptible to flaws due to incomplete information and the ingrained biases inherent to our cognition. People, news, a book, or a new thought can suddenly change our thoughts and perception of a situation.

How then can we rectify these fallacies of the mind? How can we transcend these weaknesses to unlock our innate potential and resilience? What if we constructed a reality in which our true essence triumphed over our mental fluctuations? What if we exercised restraint in our reactions, remained impervious to anger, consistently chose the path of positivity, and exuded confidence and productivity? What if we harnessed the power of our minds to our advantage, channeling it toward maximizing our productivity? What if we embraced success, and maintained a victorious attitude of positivity and happiness, even amidst external adversities? In such a state, our minds would eclipse the prowess of artificial intelligence, empowered by our control over them. In this paradigm, we could birth novel innovations, excel in both life and sports, and continue to unravel the world's challenges, now equipped with command over our minds.

However, a dilemma emerges: how do we govern our minds? How do we ascertain their value as equivalent to a billion dollars? Moreover, once control is established, can it be sustained? Can our minds transform into tools or weapons, wielded to achieve our desired outcomes?

Paradoxically, even in full cognizance of the power held within our minds, the most heightened emotional states can render individuals of exceptional mental strength vulnerable to thoughts of conflict, rage, and destruction. Consider the numerous tennis rackets shattered during matches, even by champions and elite athletes. Our minds, during the most arduous moments, can spiral into chaos. Emotions such as hunger, stress, fear, pain, sleep deprivation, financial strife, and the presence of negative influences can destabilize even the most robust minds. Regardless of the external milieu, how do we surmount these challenges and rectify the vulnerabilities and frailties of our minds?

What if, even in the face of adversity, we maintained our optimistic, triumphant outlook? In such a world, our minds would outshine even the most advanced Artificial Intelligence, spawning innovation, triumphs in endeavors, and the relentless pursuit of solutions to global challenges—because our minds would be under our dominion.

A pertinent analogy can be drawn between a robust human mind and the human body. Much attention is devoted to nourishing our bodies with wholesome diets and exercise regimens to bolster physical prowess. Similarly, let us nourish our minds with a wholesome diet of positive sensory inputs and productive outputs to optimize its functionality. Like the body, the mind necessitates regular practice and exercise to discern that the automatic thoughts we generate aren't necessarily grounded in reality. We possess the genuine capability to generate affirmative thoughts in our favor. At the close of each chapter, practical exercises will be provided to facilitate this journey.

Each Thought Has a Billion-Dollar Potential

Let's refocus on our purpose. It's evident that we remain subservient to our minds unless we master control over them. We're now aware of the remarkable potency and intricacy of the human mind. Thoughts form the bedrock of our aspirations and deeds. Now, how do we attain mastery over our minds? How can we pivot from defeat to overnight success?

Our objective is to reign in our thoughts. Through thought control, we can gain dominion over our minds and triumph over our world.

Envision every thought as a potential worth of a billion dollars. As we diligently refine our thought processes, each correct thought becomes akin to acquiring a billion dollars. Conversely, neglecting this process can steer us onto the path of failure and loss. This book is designed to heighten our awareness of mental vulnerabilities and reshape our thinking patterns, enabling us to leverage our minds to our advantage. By mastering our thoughts, we command our actions and eventual outcomes, behaviors, and emotions. This book focuses on thought control because once positive thoughts are generated, they can result in positive energy and positive behavior.

While money and looks will upgrade your lifestyle, mental strength and thoughts will upgrade you to living a great life. Make your mental thoughts your best friend. Positive thoughts are energy that can positively affect your outcomes and health.

Mental strength can help reduce stress by being able to respond to problems more easily. It can help improve joy and productivity, enabling you to reach your full potential. An adjustment of our mind and controlling our thoughts can result in infinite joy with positive outcomes which is our goal to give you.

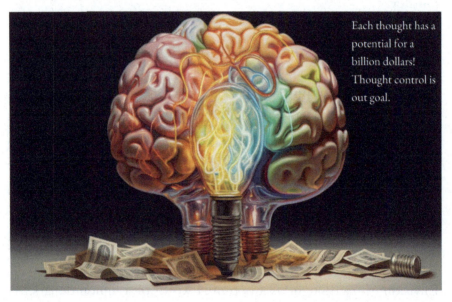

Each thought has a potential for a billion dollars! Thought control is out goal.

Take Full Responsibility For Each Thought

The human mind possesses immense power, thanks to its composition of 100 billion neurons and a staggering 100 trillion connections within the brain. Given this intricacy, it becomes paramount to program our minds in a way that favors our success. Nurturing, training, and reinforcing our minds are essential steps toward achieving our goals. However, the evolutionary facets of our minds can often veer toward fear, anxiety, negativity, or erratic and unfounded thoughts.

Understanding that thought control is a learned skill in our control, not a genetic inheritance, is truly motivating. Thus, we must dedicate ourselves to practicing this discipline daily—treating it both as an exercise and as nourishment to fortify our minds and control our thoughts.

Now we know that mind control is in our control and crucial to our next level in life, so what next? The ultimate goal of this book is to make our minds strong or resilient enough to face life's challenges. Resilience is another word for mental strength and means that the mind is able to maintain control despite the external environment. In order to build resilience or mental strength, the chapters in this book are like mental food that will fortify the mind, and create a mind so strong that will be a mental bubble without letting any outside influences or external circumstances affect it.

Mind control is in our *power* and our *choice*. Can you believe that we have so much power? We are the masters of our universe. How? We have the power to control our thoughts and how we respond to events. This makes us powerful over ourselves, our emotions, and the actions we create. Take this *power* and use it throughout the book. This book is about *responding* to events and making the mind so strong that outside influences can not and do not affect us. This ability is in our power and it's our choice. Mental resilience and strength encourage us to act without reacting.

From here onward, it will be necessary to take full responsibility for our thoughts as they are under our control. The book starts beyond self-pity. Self-pity involves feeling sorry for oneself and not only wastes time but also is an excuse for not moving forward, taking action, or improving. Self-pity can result in a negative downward spiral of negative emotions, and negative associations, thus creating negative thoughts that result in unproductive results.

A Farmer or Librarian? Our Thoughts are Easily Influenced[1]

The book "Thinking, Fast and Slow" authored by Daniel Kahneman exemplifies how our thoughts can be inherently flawed due to sudden decisions rooted in cognitive biases. Consider, for instance, a person described as shy, reserved, mild-mannered, meticulous, inclined toward details, and possessing a penchant for order and structure. Such attributes might lead one to associate this personality with a librarian rather than a farmer. However, introducing the fact that there are more farmers than librarians alters this perspective, potentially casting this personality as that of a farmer.

A Man Born with Amputated Arms and Legs Becomes a Wrestler and Climbs Mt. Kilimanjaro

Kyle Maynard was born with a rare disorder known as congenital amputation. This means his arms extend only to his elbows and his legs to his knees. Despite this disability, he has found great success in the wrestling arena, winning an ESPN Espy award for Best Athlete with a Disability. He has climbed Mt. Kilimanjaro without assistance by crawling all 19,340 feet in 10 days. He has written a best-selling book, has a documentary film, "A Fighting Chance" about him, and even had a No Excuses CrossFit gym that he owned.

How has he managed to achieve more than the average person in a single lifetime, especially with such a rare physical disability? His secret is his mind control. In his book, "No excuses, The True Story of a Congenital Amputee," he describes that you should, "never quit, never back down to anyone or anything, and to fear no challenge".[2] These words resonate with a strong resilient mind. He describes his internal mind as a "tiger's heart" that is victorious despite the external world.[3] He has a no-excuse attitude, which allows him to have full control over his mind and thoughts, not allowing any negative thoughts to interfere with his success. He uses humor, a positive attitude, gratitude, and focus—amongst other techniques described in this book—to boost his mental strength and resilience.

Alexander the Great and the Indian Yogi

There exists a widely-known tale of Alexander the Great and an Indian yogi named Dandamis. When Alexander proclaimed himself as king, the yogi retorted, asserting that Alexander was a "slave of his slave."[4] Upon delving deeper into the matter, it became apparent that the yogi was referring to Alexander's enslavement to his own anger, which the yogi had effectively mastered. Hence, the seemingly illustrious title "Great" could be replaced with "slave of anger." Our responsibility lies in not succumbing to the dominion of our minds, regardless of the extent of our wealth or achievements.

The mentally strong yogi Dandamis said: "Alexander the Great, although you proclaim yourself as a great king, you are a slave of anger, which is my slave, and thus you are a 'slave of my slave'."

Next Steps: Neuroanatomy

Given the profound complexity of the human mind, conquering it may seem intricate. We aim to simplify this process as much as possible, drawing upon foundational principles of neuroscience.

Considering that the mind is an extension of the brain and nervous system, our journey commences with an exploration of neuroanatomy—a crucial foundation that propels us toward our objective of mastering thought control.

Next Steps: Practical Exercises and Journaling Exercises

Journaling will help you get to the deepest thoughts, which is about you and your world with no rules. To upgrade your thoughts, it is important to write them down and journal them, especially with each practical exercise at the end of each chapter.

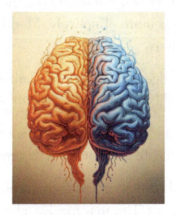

Mind control

Your mind is the center of your world,
It can make you happy or it can make you sad,
But if you can control your mind, you will be glad,
As it will take you to heights you never had.
So work on controlling your mind and thoughts every day,
You will win and perform your best in every way.

 ## Billion-Dollar Mind Exercises

As you engage with this book, keep in mind that you are embarking on a personal exploration within your own mind, guided by the following steps:

1. Identify your genuine passion.

2. Recognize mental patterns that are not conducive to your progress. Consider how you can utilize the time spent in introspection or meditation more effectively. Meditation can be done in one minute sessions.

3. Swiftly acknowledge sensory stimuli and behavioral responses that hinder you; this experience varies for each individual.

4. Cultivate robust and healthful personal sensory input and behavioral output. Advocate for yourself in this endeavor.

5. Strive for mental resilience and focus, which can propel you toward your objectives. This may involve adopting specific routines that sharpen your mind prior to events, competitions, or performances. This could include emptying your mind of negative thoughts including fear, shame, or self-doubt. Fill your thoughts with positivity, peace, love, ideas, and future goals. This will help prevent negative thoughts from entering your mind.

Exciting news! *You* have the *power* over *your mind* and *your thoughts*, and this *power* can create the life *you desire*.

Billion-Dollar Mind Journal Section

"When you have a desire, it is easy to light a fire to inspire to lift others higher."

RICK MACCI

Billion-Dollar Mind Journal Section

"Your mind is more powerful than any nuclear weapon because a mind built the weapon."

RICK MACCI

Billion-Dollar Mind Journal Section

"A powerful serve is a real weapon, but the real weapon is your mind."

RICK MACCI

Billion-Dollar Mind Journal Section

"The difference in building a world-class champion from the ground floor compared to building a world-class building starting on the ground floor is by a few inches from one ear to another. Mental strength is stronger than physical strength."

RICK MACCI

"The mind controls the body, and you control the mind."

- RICK MACCI

CHAPTER 2

Neuroanatomy Behind Thought Control

Our brains consist of a staggering 100 billion neurons. When we combine this fact with the wide spectrum of giftedness and mental health conditions, we're confronted with a challenging starting point for unraveling the intricate workings of the human mind and achieving thought control.

How can we even begin comprehending the mechanisms behind controlling our thoughts? What does the neuroanatomy reveal? Just as computer programmers work on coding our computers, this book aims to unravel the intricacies of our mental programming, commencing with the fundamentals of neuroanatomy. We'll leverage the basics and any available clues to decipher the neuronal processes influencing our thoughts, while the subsequent sections of the book will furnish strategies for mastering thought control.

The nervous system is broadly categorized into two main sections: the central nervous system, encompassing the brain and spinal cord, and the peripheral nervous system, which involves nerves. Within the peripheral nervous system, nerves can be categorized into two significant groups: motor and sensory nerves. Motor nerves facilitate the execution of actions, while sensory nerves transmit sensory information throughout the body.

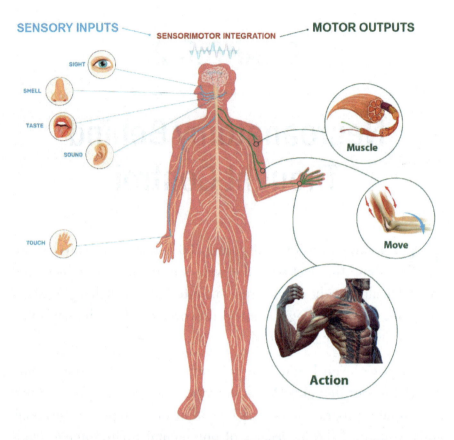

The primary input is sensory, while the key output is motor. Sensory input encompasses a diverse array of bodily sensations, whereas motor output translates into muscle movement and activity. The sensory system holds significance as it encompasses the various sensations we're acquainted with from our school days: taste, touch, smell, sound, and sight. For the body, it also encompasses the perception of touch, encompassing factors like pressure, pain, temperature, and body position.

Conversely, the motor system is responsible for executing actions. It engages motor nerves, which establish connections with muscles to initiate movement.

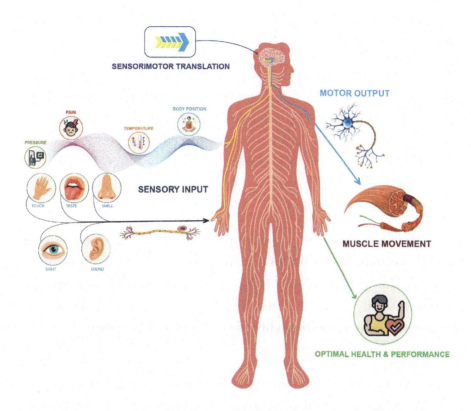

Introducing an additional layer of intricacy, situated between sensory input and motor output is the mind. While the mind is promptly engaged through our fundamental senses, these senses become ingrained in intricate memories, giving rise to matrices or thought patterns and responses that subsequently influence our actions. The mind is an intricate entity composed of sensory input that triggers a cascade of thoughts, memories, and emotions (operating within our limbic system). When contemplating how neuroanatomy influences thought and mind control, it's important to consider sensory inputs and motor outputs.

Optimizing our Thoughts Through our Senses via the Sensory Nervous System

Delving into the realm of senses, let's take the sense of smell as an example. Controlled by the olfactory nerve (cranial nerve one), smell signals are conveyed to the olfactory bulb, situated at the frontal part of the brain. Given its location, scents directly engage with the limbic system, including the amygdala and hippocampus, swiftly triggering emotions and memories. Hence, scents can swiftly forge a connection with the mind.

Other sensations follow a similar pathway. This sense of smell can evoke positivity and confidence when associated with positive memories or thoughts. Similarly, taste can be enhanced through specific foods, fostering a positive mindset. For example, a sweet taste can generate feelings and thoughts of positivity and happiness.[5]

Touch can be amplified through the texture of particular clothing, soft objects, or even interacting with a kitten or dog, inducing positive thoughts and ultimately a sense of happiness that yields positive outcomes. Touch is a powerful tool; a warm embrace or soft touch can elicit thoughts of trust, gratitude, sympathy, love, and cooperation. Even brief touches during a team sport like basketball can improve team performance.[6]

Visual stimuli involving the sense of sight are equally pivotal; observing something pleasant externally and visualizing it internally can lead to positive outcomes.

Music is a universal expression that uses the sense of hearing to impact our brain, improving our mood and emotion. Music has the power to bring us to tears or motivate us to do our best.[7] Music can help release neurotransmitters such as dopamine leading to a pleasurable feeling.[8] Listening to a particular song can also cultivate a confident, positive mindset, evident in practices or pep rallies that channel sensory input to focus the mind in a positive direction.

Our bodies favor specific senses that generate positive emotions, necessitating our awareness of these sensations and actions that generate positive thoughts.

Optimizing our Thoughts Through our Actions via the Motor Nervous System

Having explored how the sensory nervous system brings sensations to our awareness, let's consider the motor aspect. Can our thoughts be influenced by carrying out motor actions, gestures, or engaging in actions? Yes. Engaging in acts of gratitude, maintaining a positive attitude, practicing self-discipline, self-improvement, concentration, and focus all contribute to cultivating mental strength and thought control. A motor action not only reflects a thought, but can also provide feedback to the mind, thereby generating thoughts of empowerment and positivity.

Optimal functioning of our minds hinges on the synchronization of correct sensory input and motor output, where even seemingly minor actions can exert a significant long-term impact on mental resilience.

A crucial point to remember is that mastery of sensory input and motor output serves as the key to cultivating a billion-dollar mind.

Our sensations are diverse, infiltrating memory and emotion, culminating in specific actions. By regulating sensory input, we can better steer our minds and actions. Similarly, when we enact appropriate motor actions, we direct the generation of our thoughts through those actions. And remember, this journey is deeply personal—sensory input and motor output elicit individual responses.

Parasympathetic and Sympathetic Nervous System Effects on Thoughts.

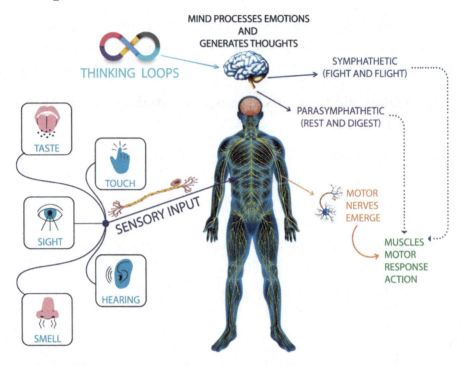

Our final layer of complexity involves the interplay between the mind and the sympathetic and parasympathetic nervous systems, which work together to harmonize emotions and actions. These nervous systems operate autonomically and automatically. Their significance lies in their role in instigating actions.

When the body is tense or anxious, the sympathetic system is triggered, preparing the body for fight or flight responses, causing a heightened state of nervous system tension.

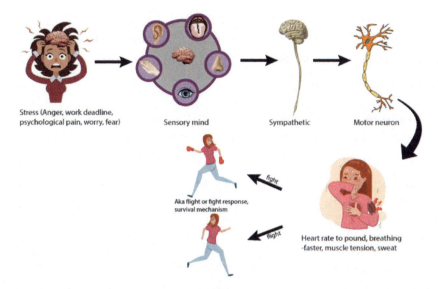

On the other hand, when the body is at ease or engaged in activities like eating, the parasympathetic nervous system comes into play.

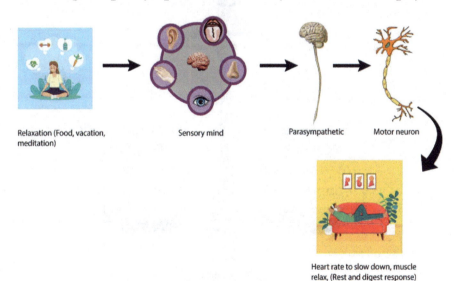

How do the parasympathetic and sympathetic nervous systems connect with our previous discussion? These two systems, the parasympathetic and sympathetic nervous systems, play a role in translating thoughts into motor responses automatically. It's important to acknowledge that our thoughts can impact these systems; stressful thoughts might lead to muscle tension, whereas relaxing thoughts can promote muscle relaxation. Maintaining awareness of our thoughts is essential.

For optimal performance, ideal performance state[9], it's crucial that the parasympathetic nervous system counterbalances the sympathetic system, creating a balance between alertness and relaxation. Engaging the parasympathetic nervous system could involve practices like deep breathing and smiling before a competition while thinking about the competition might activate the sympathetic nervous system.

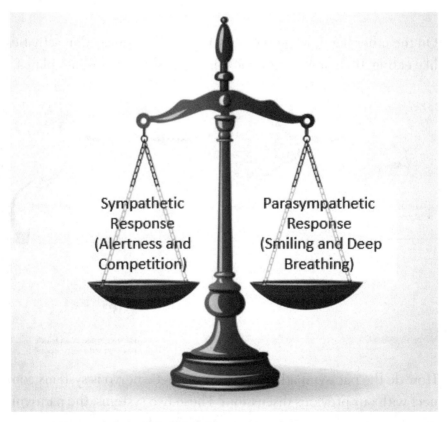

> **Fun Fact!**
>
> When you are playing tennis or in a stressful situation, **smile** and **deep breathe** to help balance the parasympathetic and sympathetic nervous systems.

Why Everyone Should Smile More

Smiling can help reduce the sympathetic stress response of the muscles and result in a relaxed state. This was evidenced by a 2018 research study with researchers at Ulster University and Swansea University in which 24 runners who smiled more were using less oxygen and were 2.8% more efficient compared to those who frowned and those who were neither frowning nor smiling.[10] In fact, top-ranked marathon runner, Eliud Kipchoge who has achieved world records in marathons, smiles intentionally to relax and help endure the pain.[11]

In life as well as in running, smiling can help make things easier, make you feel more positive, and also make you look better. Smiling reduces the sympathetic system response of flight and fight and also allows the brain to release endorphins, dopamine, and serotonin, all resulting in reduced anxiety and increased happiness.

Some of the most successful and famous people have the most charming smile. Think of your favorite actor and reflect on their smile. Even a fake smile can put you in a good mood. Smiling can have a huge influence on your thoughts, mood, energy, stress, and overall health. Dr. Niva's mom always says that a smile can be the easiest and least expensive makeup on your face.

Voluntary Deep Breathing Can Help Control Your Thoughts

Deep breathing is one thing almost all professional athletes and top performers do to help control thoughts, anxiety, and stress. A 2023 study done in Italy suggested that deep breathing can help athletes improve focus and concentration. [12]

Deep breathing can benefit athletes as well as non-athletes as it balances the stress response from the sympathetic system. Deep breathing can help optimize cardiac function, reduce anxiety, and maintain focus during training and competition.

Back to the Basics: Physical Exercise, Sleep, and Massage

Studies have shown that both physical exercise (sympathetic nervous system) and sleep (parasympathetic nervous system) can affect our thinking. Although we've discussed the sensory and motor aspects of mental strength, the basics of what impacts our thinking must not be overlooked. It is known that better sleep is associated with better control of emotions and positive emotions.[13] Physical activity can also improve sleep quality. [14] Regular exercise (30 minutes total of moderate intensity for three days a week) can result in a positive mood, improve self-esteem, and thinking amongst many other things. [15] In addition to exercise and sleep, massage can reduce stress and improve mood by increasing serotonin and dopamine. [16]

 ## Billion-Dollar Mind Exercises

1. Allocate some moments for introspection and contemplate what brings you joy.

2. Jot down the flavor of a meal that brought you utmost happiness, the song that lifted your spirits, a cherished fragrance, a touch you long to experience again, captivating sounds, evoking emotions, memories that warm your heart, and visualizations that bring a smile to your face.

3. Utilize these sensations daily to shape the finest version of yourself.

4. Practice taking a deep breath during a stressful situation to help control your thoughts and bring relaxation.

5. Practice smiling in the mirror 10-15 times a day to bring positive thoughts and emotions.

 **Billion-Dollar Mind Journal Section**

"It can be little things in life-soft touch, a smile, our own thoughts, and love that can provide comfort and are important to our mental health."

DR. NIVA

Billion-Dollar Mind Journal Section

"Having the ability to smile when you do not want to is a skill that the best of the best master."

RICK MACCI

Billion-Dollar Mind Journal Section

"Breathe out when you hit and you'll be a breath of fresh air."

RICK MACCI

Billion-Dollar Mind Journal Section

"Calmness and intensity are the ultimate combination in competition."

RICK MACCI

BILLION-DOLLAR MIND

"You control the situation. Do not let the situation control you."

-RICK MACCI

CHAPTER 3

Thinking Loops are Traps

Now that we're aware of the presence of motor and sensory inputs in our thoughts, along with the involvement of the parasympathetic and sympathetic systems, we are now confronted with one of the most significant hurdles in our thought process: **thinking loops**.

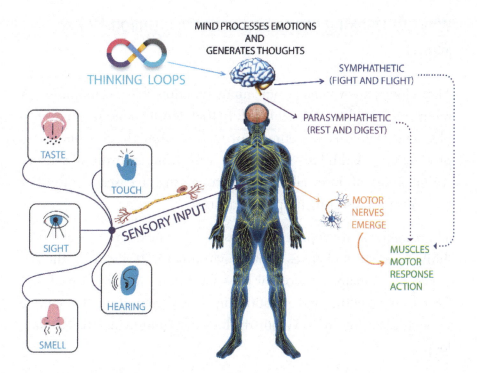

What are Thinking Loops?

Thinking loops consist of thought patterns ingrained in us from upbringing. These thoughts are extensive and can impact decisions, behaviors, outcomes, and success. Overcoming these loops is akin to scaling Mt. Everest, yet, grappling with thinking loops is a personal journey, as thoughts often intertwine with complex past patterns that can hinder desired outcomes. The journey to creating new thought patterns starts with recognition, followed by detachment. Perhaps it entails releasing a cultural belief that might set you apart from others but liberate you to achieve your aspirations. It's essential to analyze each thought objectively, questioning its validity, helpfulness, and necessity.

Why are Thinking Loops Important to a Billion-Dollar Mind?

These loops are crucial as our minds function akin to computers. A recurring thought or thought pattern that doesn't benefit you resembles a mental virus, affecting your mental strength, efficiency, and productivity. A thinking loop might arise from an external sensory stimulus or an internal thought, triggering a cascade of other thoughts and resulting in specific actions.

Thinking loops are connected to resilience, which is the mental flexibility to adapt to changes in our environment. Resilience is the key to success in many areas of our lives and can result in improved performance, health, and relationships. It's important to mental strength. We can improve our resilience by improving our thinking loops.

Resilience Increases with Conquering Thinking Loops

Consider all of the potential difficulties in life: work-related issues, failed relationships, struggles with health, or success in achieving your personal and professional goals. Our thinking patterns are how we view every obstacle and how we respond to it. The more resilient we are, the easier it will be to overcome obstacles, failures, struggles, and stop negativity, anxiety, and doubt. You have the ability to do this and this section will equip you with some tools to help improve resilience.

For instance, an internal thought of anxiety can lead to bodily tension, while a thought of happiness can induce relaxation. The following thinking loop illustrates how negative sensory inputs can impact motor performance and yield suboptimal outcomes.

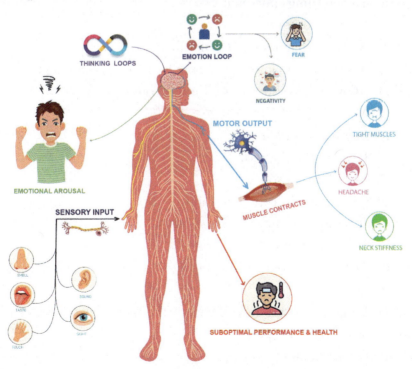

Even though resilience can have multiple components to it, an important component of building resilience is to recognize our thought patterns. This involves observing our thoughts when there is a challenge. Once you observe your thoughts, you have to be keen to observe the subsequent thoughts or the domino effect of the thoughts that one thought generates.

Here are some thinking loop traps:

1. Self-blame for everything
2. Anxiety when you think about the future
3. Comparing yourself to others
4. False long-held beliefs
5. Making a conclusion immediately with no data
6. Focusing on the negative
7. Taking things personally
8. Blaming others
9. Always explaining and generalizing
10. Assuming you know what someone else is thinking
11. Allowing emotions to predict the outcome
12. Not being open to change
13. Pleasing everyone
14. Dwelling in the past
15. Repeating mistakes
16. Giving up after the first failure
17. Resenting other people's success
18. Fear and fear of being alone
19. The world owes you something
20. Self-pity
21. Family or loved one's advice is the best advice; consider advice from an expert
22. Overthinking

Keys to freeing yourself from these traps include self-reflection, spending time with your thoughts, awareness, flexibility, gaining more knowledge, and open-mindedness.

Conquering a Tragic Thinking Loop

Sheryl Sandberg, Facebook COO, lost her husband, David Goldberg due to a tragic incident when he was 47. They were vacationing in Mexico and he was exercising when he suddenly collapsed and passed away from a cardiac arrhythmia. Although devastating and painful, the event was handled with such intelligence and thought. Not only did Sheryl Sandberg write a book about "Option B: Facing Adversity, Building Resilience and Finding Joy"[17] with Adam Grant, but she also describes how she reframed the situation and depressing thinking loop so it would become less painful. Instead of focusing on the loss, there was a thought about how it could have been worse if her husband had suffered the cardiac arrhythmia while driving the kids. She reframed her thoughts from pain to gratitude, being able to appreciate that she still had her kids and she should be grateful for what she still has.

Misunderstandings with Others

Every day we can find faults and insignificant misunderstandings with other people whether it involves an invitation, phone call, polite expression, greeting, gift, or any sort of expectation. You can get caught up with these thoughts and then start to develop resentment all due to a misunderstanding or misinterpretation of an event. Follow patterns of your behavior and recognize that if you have certain relationship patterns, try to fix thinking traps with them. Ask yourself questions if you have overreacted and stick to the facts. Opening up your concerns can be helpful. Forgiving, forgetting, letting go, understanding, and removing negative interpretations or misunderstandings can help build a billion-dollar mind as well as result in a better outcome in the long run.

For example, if there are two coworkers who dislike each other, we must realize that our own dislikes and likes are the cause of our own problems. It is our own mind that is the problem rather than the other person. Once we adopt a nonjudgmental, open mind with acceptance as well as change our way of thinking, we stop wanting the other person to change.[18]

 **Billion-Dollar Mind Exercises**

1. Throughout your day, take a moment to reflect on your emotions. If you find yourself experiencing sadness or self-inflicted pain that hinders your daily activities or pursuit of your dreams, take a closer look at the thoughts driving those emotions.

2. Identify the recurring thinking loop that's contributing to your own distress and examine it from various angles.

3. Shifting your perspective on a thought can diminish its significance. For instance, if someone you value has hurt you, try viewing them from multiple viewpoints. What do their family and friends think of them? Is this person truly the right presence in your life? Are you genuinely content with their role? Are they as sincere as they appear? What are their strengths and weaknesses? Are there aspects of their personality they haven't revealed? As you become more aware and expand your understanding of a particular thinking loop, you'll find that it begins to dissolve.

Billion-Dollar Mind Journal Section

"The story we tell ourselves determines whether we succeed or fail in life!"

DR. NIVA

Billion-Dollar Mind Journal Section

"To get to the mountain top, you have to go slow, look both ways, be careful, make adjustments, and do not look back."

RICK MACCI

Billion-Dollar Mind Journal Section

"Conquering our vast, intricate thinking loops is equivalent to climbing Mt Everest."

DR. NIVA

Billion-Dollar Mind Journal Section

"Players who say 'I can't' won't."

RICK MACCI

"Every day you feed your face with food. Feed your brain with positive words and the food will taste even better!"

— RICK MACCI

CHAPTER 4

Sensory Mental Diet and Exercise: Positive Thoughts

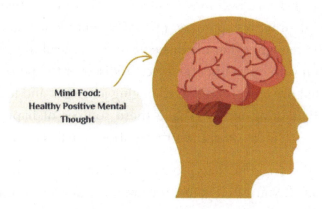

Isn't it ironic that our brains are inherently inclined towards negativity, yet positivity is the cornerstone of success?

This may be hardwired as a survival mechanism but can hinder our mental power and thought control. Whenever we capture a moment or engage in an activity with others, our minds immediately gravitate towards the one aspect that may have gone awry or appeared imperfect, rather than acknowledging the multitude of things that went right.

Our natural inclination is to lean towards negativity. Negativity serves only to undermine your authentic self and provoke your inner voice into turmoil, disturbing your inner peace. Embracing negativity is a sure path towards failure.

Simultaneously, a negative thought can be transformed into a positive one, triggering a shift in our overall mood, outlook, energy, and productivity. Through the use of positive affirmations, your mind can establish a more positive baseline state. Positive way, positive results, think about your goals, results and get what you want and you will become more positive and be in control of your life.

The word "thought" comes from old English and it means to conceive in the mind. Thoughts serve as the foundational building blocks of our success. Without constructive thoughts, the path to achieving anything becomes challenging. It's imperative that our thoughts align with happiness, positivity, confidence, and success. When our thoughts veer off this course, it's crucial to reestablish a connection with our authentic selves, rediscover the powerful motivations that drive us through challenging journeys, and focus on endeavors that bring us joy. While these sources of happiness may differ for each individual, their recognition remains paramount.

Monitor the triggers that prompt negative or despondent states within you. If you catch yourself expressing negativity, engaging in unproductive activities, or experiencing a lack of motivation, consider these occurrences from the perspectives of hunger, fatigue, insufficient physical activity, or a lack of balance.

Positive thinking works not only in life's success but also in healthier lives and relationships. People become happier in life. All of us have negative situations or obstacles; it is how we respond to these obstacles that make us turn a negative into a positive. Each problem is short lived and staying positive will eventually allow good things to happen. Being positive is limitless! Be as positive as possible and you will also attract positive, upbeat enthusiastic people.

Dr. Niva's Tennis Career to a Medical Career: Achieved with the Guidance of the Right Coach

I couldn't find a tennis coach that matched my desires during this time. I was always searching but never found the ideal coach. The coaches I came across had a fault in some way, and we didn't mesh. They were either unenthusiastic, jaded, provided poor instructions, or lacked the passion I possessed. I quickly learned the tennis scene in Florida or Georgia did not fit me. The only way I could learn tennis was through tennis magazines or instruction on TV and videos. It wasn't an ideal way of learning. It seemed I would never find a coach, but fate intervened, giving me one of the best tennis coaches in the world.

I played in a national tournament in Florida and my opponent was highly esteemed, mostly due to their coach. I wasn't familiar with the coach's name at the time, but the people around me in Florida considered him an elite coach. In the end, I won the match and returned home. It wasn't long before I received a letter in the mail from Rick Macci, the man who had coached my opponent at the national tournament in Florida. I wondered how he had tracked me down. Rick was one of the few coaches to reach out to me. Once I talked to him, I found him to be focused and intelligent. I had finally found the right tennis coach to help me reach the next level.

I joined his academy in South Florida and immediately began to learn. My journal was full of information from each day. I just marveled at the honesty, sincerity, extreme kindness, genuineness, and passion Rick and his team had to make tennis players better.

Rick was extremely charismatic, kind, and personable. I never heard him get upset even once no matter the situation. He had an aura of positivity that surprised me. I will never forget a Sunday after a massive rainstorm when I was told to jog laps outside while the courts dried. I did it dutifully. I mumbled to myself, "I am sure Rick Macci is not here. I am sure he has gone home like every other coach." Then, I glanced to my right and saw a faraway image of Rick training a student to run up and down hills. I couldn't believe that a coach like him could exist. I have never stopped trusting him or appreciating him since then.

There were a few very important lessons I learned from being his student. One was to cringe when I heard the word vanilla. I still do not eat anything vanilla. Vanilla meant average. It was something that would never get you anywhere. I also learned that my positivity could be exponentially increased when I saw him. I could only be more positive in life because there was no limit to it. I would also wonder how he could start earlier than me even though my training started at 7:30 a.m. I could barely get to the court in those days after long hours of training and he was starting as early as 4:00 a.m., with so much energy. It made me so motivated and competitive. I recognized he was someone I could look up to as a player and as a person.

As a junior player the greatest impact Rick had on me was his ability to decrease my fear of coming to the net. He would also tease me saying that girls fear the net. I remember going into my matches, hearing those words in my head, and it would be such a challenge for me to come to the net, but I firmly decided not to be afraid. I had a lot of confidence since I was seeded number 1 in almost every tournament. So, I started going to the net in some of my matches and started winning more quickly and easily. Rick also taught me about honesty. If I wasn't going to be a top player on the pro tour, it was important to change direction in a field that I could master. His lessons changed my life.

And I never felt alone with Rick around. I am allergic to average. I run away from it and it's hard to be alone working hard, being obsessed with maximizing my impact on this world. I've struggled to be alone all my life—surrounded by 99.9% of the people who are okay with average thinking, eating, personal fitness, habits, and goals.

It took me years to understand that I would lower my standards to connect and then get frustrated because no one seemed to understand excellence and I could never understand them. Why do people want to watch hundreds of hours of TV? Why do people major in minors? Why are people so negative? Why don't people want to work hard and be amazing?

Rick was the first person I met who was not average and always worked harder than me with so much awesomeness, success, and consistency. It felt great to be around him. Noticing how my sister and I would study during breaks, Rick wrote a very sweet handwritten note for us to get into Harvard.

He is just a magnanimous person to be around and elevates everyone around him. No one can even imagine how much he has gone through. It would probably destroy the average person if they went through 1% of what Rick has experienced. He is strong in every way.

Rick Macci is the champion of champions! When training alongside someone like Rick Macci or another dedicated professional, feelings of isolation fade, replaced by inspiration. The journey toward success can indeed feel lonely at times, as the pursuit of excellence often demands more effort than the norm.

Leaders who strive for greatness are distinguishable from followers who opt for complacency, lethargy, and unhealthy habits. Rick Macci's commitment to training, rain or shine, contrasts starkly with other coaches who retreat at the first sign of bad weather. An athlete committed to high performance thrives in adversity and remains undeterred by rain. Effective coaches and positive associations are essential pillars in developing a successful, productive mindset.

Positive Thoughts

Positive Thoughts, Positive Thoughts, Positive Thoughts,
These are diamonds that can't be bought.
Positive Thoughts, Positive Thoughts, Positive Thoughts,
These are mental weapons to be taught.
Positive Thoughts, Positive Thoughts, Positive Thoughts,
These are daily self-generated miracles to be sought.
Positive Thoughts, Positive Thoughts, Positive Thoughts,
If you have them, you will win a whole lot.

 ## Billion-Dollar Mind Exercises

1. Consistently observe the thoughts you generate and whether they lean towards negativity or positivity. Record these thoughts and take time to assess why a particular thought arises, either hourly or daily as needed. When negativity emerges, actively identify its source and eliminate it. Understand that these negative thoughts lack validity, and by pinpointing their causes, you can remove them from your mental landscape. Recognizing recurring thought patterns permits you to introspect on your weaknesses and anticipate your future responses to challenges.

2. Frequent practice is key to eradicating unproductive thought patterns, such as doubts, anxieties, fears, and other negative influences that hinder your progress toward the next level of success.

3. You might write these thoughts down, but as you immerse yourself in a positive state, address negative thoughts promptly by identifying their root causes and swiftly eliminating them.

4. Negative thoughts have the potential to trigger the sympathetic nervous system's fight-or-flight response, leading to muscle tension. Therefore, vigilance in monitoring such thoughts is crucial. When you notice negative thoughts surfacing, acknowledge their presence, erase them, and engage in deep breathing to recenter your focus on the present moment

5. The concept of "tree bathing" involves purging your mind of self-generated negativity, doubts, fears, worries, anxiety, and grudges while surrounded by trees or nature. In this serene environment, you can foster positive thoughts while simultaneously discarding detrimental ones, contributing to a rejuvenated mindset.

Billion-Dollar Mind Journal Section

"It's easy to get really upset, so stay positive to avoid the real upset."

RICK MACCI

Billion-Dollar Mind Journal Section

"When you totally understand that the best of the best of all the rest are the most positive creatures with this mindset if you change you will have no regret."

RICK MACCI

Billion-Dollar Mind Journal Section

"Train your mind every day to be positive."

RICK MACCI

BILLION-DOLLAR MIND

"The best gas to fill up your tank is not at the fuel pump. It is you pumping positive thoughts in your tank. The best fuel to have more energy is to avoid negative people."

-RICK MACCI

CHAPTER 5

Sensory Mental Diet and Exercise: Positive Associations

What are Positive Associations?

Association comes from the Latin word, *associate*, which means to unite and ally. Positive associations are positive, motivating individuals who uplift and inspire, propelling you to reach your highest potential. These are people whom you aspire to be like or who have qualities you desire. These are people who make things happen for you and say yes instead of no. These are people who help you achieve your dreams and make you feel positive, happy, energetic, and uplifted. If someone makes you feel otherwise, even by the slightest percentage, then they can hold you back from achieving your dreams and the next level of your life. A positive association is someone who matches your energy and will help you win.

Sometimes it is challenging to find people who match you completely. People have positive and negative qualities, so people will be positive at times and negative at other times. The most important gauge in determining their impact on your life is the energy they leave behind and how they make you feel. Do they encourage you to start achieving your dreams and do you feel inspired by them or do they make you feel sad, depressed, and negative? This feeling will be critical in evaluating whether the association is positive or not.

In addition, be attentive to the words directed at you. Criticism, if not managed, can chip away at motivation and enthusiasm, plunging you into a cycle of self-defeating thoughts that breed inefficiency, demotivation, and even depression.

Why are Positive Associations Important to a Billion-Dollar Mind?

Positive associations provide positive sensory input to the brain thus making them crucial in reaching a positive state that will allow you to reach the next level of your life. Transforming your environment, thought patterns, and beliefs with positive associations, triggers a shift in your entire world. Your life will be filled with fresh ideas and effective actions, propelling you to new levels.

Investing in quality relationships is crucial. The reason for prioritizing quality people is evident in moments like these. A single negative remark or suggestion can trigger a cascade of detrimental thoughts and emotions, derailing progress and focus.

The following experience serves as a reminder that feedback is valuable only when it's constructive and aligned with your goals.

Example of Positive Associations in Life: Dr. Niva's Personal Story

One Saturday afternoon, as I went about my routine activities, my phone rang. It was a call from a family member, who, though well-intentioned, began to express concerns about my social circle and the principles I followed. She mentioned that some of these principles might not be considered "cool." I calmly responded, explaining my selective approach to friendships and how the pursuit of success may not always appear glamorous, but the rewards of winning and being the best certainly are. Despite her caring tone, her words held a tinge of negativity.

Shortly after, another call came in, this time with criticism from within the family. There were remarks about the kids needing more activities and reminders about applying sunscreen. Then, a third call arrived, accompanied by more family criticism. It seemed that something needed to be ordered online, and I had not been informed until that moment.

In the midst of working on this book and my personal growth, I noticed a shift in my initial response. Although my mind was tempted to veer into negativity—thoughts of not being liked, doubts about the effectiveness of these principles, and confusion about orders—I caught myself. I realized that negative input from others could sap my confidence, enthusiasm, and drive for success.

I sought refuge in lectures with positive messages and the support of friends who consistently shared uplifting content. This infusion of positive energy helped restore my usual highly productive, positive, and happy state. I consciously fed myself a diet of quality positivity.

Positive Associations

Be around someone who inspires and encourages you,
This will help your dreams come true.
They will teach you things you never knew,
And you will be one amongst the few.
The right friends bring positivity and happiness,
And inspire you to your best.
So choose carefully who is close to you,
Make sure they are positive, kind, caring, and true.

 ## Billion-Dollar Mind Exercises

1. Just as you make choices to reduce high-sugar or high-fat foods in your diet, make a conscious effort to limit your exposure to negative individuals. When interactions are necessary, allocate only a specific amount of time and energy for engaging with their responses. When you anticipate a conversation with them—whether it's answering their call or engaging in a dialogue—foresee that negativity and criticism might arise. This preemptive awareness will detach you from taking their remarks personally.

2. Swiftly identify negative influences and create distance, both physically and mentally. Counteract their negative energy with self-love, maintaining the health and productivity of your mind.

3. Additionally, observe their recurrent patterns of negativity not only in your interactions but also in their exchanges with others. This broader perspective further distances their negativity from affecting your emotions. Respond with positivity, self-assuredness, and a smile. Explore whether you can be of assistance to them, while maintaining your own sense of well-being.

4. Acknowledge their critique and consider using it constructively if applicable. If it doesn't align with your goals, remain focused on your objectives.

5. If their negativity still lingers and impacts your mindset, try a therapeutic approach. Jot down their remarks on paper, then symbolically release their influence by tearing up the paper and discarding it. Keep in mind that their negativity might linger and resurface during future interactions. Minimize your exposure to

such interactions whenever possible to protect your mindset and maintain your momentum toward success.

6. Surround yourself with positive energy and positive people; if you can't find them, connect with positivity through videos and books.

Negative comments from someone

Domino of negative thoughts

Go down hill into a bundle of negativity

Billion-Dollar Mind Journal Section

*"When you **Change** your perspective, it is a game **Changer**."*

RICK MACCI

Billion-Dollar Mind Journal Section

"Fill your life with those that inspire you, not those that tire you! Negativity and Positivity in people can be contagious, so choose carefully!"

DR. NIVA

Billion-Dollar Mind Journal Section

"Books and videos allow you to surround yourself with amazing people and their ideas!"

DR. NIVA

Billion-Dollar Mind Journal Section

> *"If you can follow greatness in other sports and see how they handle failure and see how they handle problems, there's a constant theme across the board. They're amazingly positive. They don't get too high, they don't get too low, pretty much on a regular basis. If they do get upset it makes them more determined. They don't even want to be around the negativity, so they're making a choice..."[19]*
>
> RICK MACCI

BILLION-DOLLAR MIND

"Practice in your mind first. See it, feel it, and then do it. Dream it, feel it, smell it, touch it long before you even try it."

- RICK MACCI

CHAPTER 6

Sensory Mental Diet and Exercise: Visualization

What is Visualization?

Visualization comes from the Latin word, *visus*, which means sight. Visualization is the practice of thinking in visual images and in imagination rather than in words. Visualization forms a mental image or intention of a desired outcome. A picture can be more powerful than a thousand words. Visualization engages the power of imagination to create mental images, sensations, responses, and emotions that align with desired experiences.

Visualization plays a pivotal role in achieving success by profoundly influencing the sensory system. Remarkably, it can activate the brain's motor cortex on its own. This means that even without physical execution, visualization can trigger the brain and establish new neural connections that contribute to better motor performance. For individuals with weakened motor abilities, visualizing movements can activate motor neurons, effectively strengthening them.

Incorporating visualization entails envisioning future scenarios such as how to handle pressure, relaxation, and skill mastery.

The scenarios can involve visualizing oneself as composed, poised, and exuding a champion-like aura in a pressure situation. This involves projecting an image of being a leader and champion by maintaining an upright posture and concealing negative emotions, even in high-stress situations. It involves smelling, tasting, hearing, feeling, and performing a certain action, especially during visualization of a certain performance or skill mastery. Visualizing yourself as calm and relaxed can help you achieve an optimal physical state during a competition. This mental exercise fosters self-assuredness and self-control, ensuring that you maintain composure and confidence both before and during performances.

Much research has been devoted to visualization. Visualization can be beneficial in performance and is a superpower. The human brain can have difficulty distinguishing reality from imagination, so Olympians frequently rely on visualization as a major part of their training. [20]

Why is Visualization Important to a Billion-Dollar Mind?

Visualization activates the same motor inputs and sensory inputs as the action itself. It is invaluable across various domains, including athletic and professional engagements. It clarifies actions and pairs them with positive emotions such as confidence. Integrating visualization into your daily routine can significantly enhance overall performance as it can replace anxious or fearful thoughts with positive successful thoughts about a future performance.

Mastering Chess in a Siberian Prison

Natan Sharansky's remarkable story is a prime example of the power of visualization.. He was a human rights activist who supported the rights of Jews to move to Israel and was subsequently sentenced in 1977 to jail in a Siberian prison on a false charge that he was spying on the Americans. While he spent nine years in prison, he was locked in a punishment cell without food and only a bare minimum of clothing. He had been a chess prodigy as a child, and while in prison he started to recall games in his head. He played thousands of games of chess in his imagination and became mentally stronger. Despite being cramped in a four-foot by three-foot cell for 400 days, he visualized defeating the world chess champion. When he was released, he did eventually beat the world chess champion all due to visualization in his mind. [21]

Visualization to Promote Neurological Recovery

Visualization is not only powerful in our day-to-day lives, athletics, and building inner strength during the most difficult of times, but it's also a powerful tool that can be used in the medical field.

After a stroke or a neurological disorder, patients suffer from a loss of function and limited mobility. The nervous system can recover with the help of neuroplasticity, which involves mechanisms that rewire the brain. The visualization of completing a motor task can help strengthen connections in the motor circuitry in the brain by activating these motor circuits to perform the task just by thinking about it and visualization is used in physical therapy. [22]

Visualizing Shooting Basketballs Can Improve Accuracy

A notable example is an experiment at the University of Chicago that demonstrated how visualizing shooting free throws in basketball, even without physical practice, led to an improvement in free throw accuracy.[23]

Visualization: Dreams as a Child

Rick Macci remembers stories as to how Venus and Serena Williams, who were both number one tennis players in the world, would play with dolls and imagine winning major tennis tournaments.

Visualization

When I see an image of victory in my head,
I sometimes fill myself with doubt and dread.
Could this be me?
Do I deserve victory?
And then I suddenly realize,
That this is my prize.
And without a tool like visualization,
I will be unprepared like I am on vacation.
I need to get ready mentally,
So, thoughts of executing take me close to victory.
Even when people can't move much and are weak,
Visualizations can help activate neurons to help them peak.
Visualization is a magical tool,
Most winners make it a rule.
You will be clever,
If you put your visualization in your mental power toolbox forever.

 ## Billion-Dollar Mind Exercises

1. Dedicate a portion of each day to visualize the upcoming day, envisioning how you'll respond to both anticipated patterns and unexpected situations. Approach this practice as if you're watching a vivid movie in your mind, engaging all your senses: smell, touch, taste, sound, and sight. Embrace the experience fully.

2. Document your aspirations for the coming month, five years, and ten years—covering aspects such as your career, family, home, vehicle, and financial abundance. This process will encourage your subconscious mind to work towards these envisioned goals.

3. Make visualization a daily routine, much like exercising a muscle that needs consistent practice. Select a quiet setting devoid of distractions, and visualize with intricate detail. Engage all your senses during this process, and immerse yourself in the mental images. Enhance your practice by creating visual aids like pictures, sketches, or even videos to supplement your visualization efforts.

4. Before a competition, relive a winning performance and experience the feeling of winning under pressure. Visualize the shots you want to optimize and patterns of play that you want to create. Create a mental movie of your performance successfully and then turn it into reality.

Billion-Dollar Mind Journal Section

"One positive thought can make all the difference."

DR. NIVA

Billion-Dollar Mind Journal Section

"I just hated to lose, but losing made me more determined. I also always dreamed a lot. I visualized a lot. I pictured a lot of things in my mind before I would do it. I was a very creative kid and I had a lot of energy and motivation and just loved the bright lights. Why? I'm not sure. I think when you love doing something you do whatever you can to be the best you can be and you just add layers of the big time to make it more exciting." [24]

RICK MACCI

___
___
___
___
___
___
___
___
___
___
___
___
___
___
___
___
___
___

Billion-Dollar Mind Journal Section

"Picture in your mind before it happens."

RICK MACCI

BILLION-DOLLAR MIND

"The best advice you will ever hear is when you say positive things to yourself and listen."

- RICK MACCI

CHAPTER 7

Sensory Mental Diet and Exercise: Self-love

Self-love means to have a strong value for your own well-being and happiness. It entails appreciating and valuing your own worth. This is a fundamental aspect of mental strength, involving the ability to maintain a positive self-perception even amidst negative surroundings or circumstances. It's crucial to uphold a positive self-view and maintain a sense of value regardless of challenges. Avoid diminishing your self-worth, particularly after facing setbacks, as this can lead to a downward spiral of negativity. A lack of self-love can interfere with the ability to love others.

Cultivating self-love involves embracing your passions and connecting with your inner self. This inner essence may find joy in activities like exercise, dance, yoga, specific foods, clothing, or interactions with particular individuals. Recognizing, cherishing, and respecting this core identity forms the foundation for mental resilience. Honesty with yourself and the exploration of your true nature are pivotal steps towards achieving success. This process helps you align with your authentic self, identify your goals, and fortify your mind. Once you have a clear understanding of your desires and identity, external influences become less necessary in decision-making.

Take Rick Macci, for instance, who chooses to stay rooted at his tennis academy instead of extensive travel with his professional players. His self-awareness and alignment with his preferences guide his decisions.

Integral aspects of self-love encompass acknowledging imperfections and refraining from unfavorable self-comparisons. It's easy to fall into the trap of self-defeat by allowing negativity to arise through social media comparisons or self-deprecating thoughts.

Find yourself. Connect with yourself. Put yourself first. Don't put others first to your own detriment.

The greatest champions knew they would be number one in the world, committed their life to excellence, and loved and believed in themselves.

A Tennis Player Who Loves Himself So Much That He Never Wants to Change His Physical Limitations [25] [26]

Roger Crawford, a motivational speaker, was born with a condition that left him with one finger on his right hand, two on his left hand, a missing left leg, and two toes on his right side. His parents refused to let him pity himself, so he was determined to play tennis because he fell in love with it. He found a racket that fit his grip and spent hours hitting against a wall. Reoger worked so hard that he started winning against players who didn't have a disability and he even went on to play in a Division one school, the first to compete with a disability in the NCAA. He didn't give up and noticed opportunities in obstacles. Roger loves to motivate and inspire others. He states that he wouldn't change his physical limitations, because he would have to give up the incredible blessings he has had because of them.

Self-love

Having self-love,
Is a true gift from above.
Being loved by others is so fun,
But true self-love is a home run.
There's no one that can understand you or match you,
Other than your true you.
So, recognize how beautiful and wonderful it is to be,
Lost in the love of your own company.

 ## Billion-Dollar Mind Exercises

1. Write down 10 aspects you genuinely appreciate about yourself. If any negative self-perceptions arise, jot them on the paper and promptly tear it up. Remind yourself: "I grant myself forgiveness for any mistakes." Embrace the opportunity to learn from missteps and constructive feedback, but shield your self-love from being compromised by these experiences.

2. Intentional thoughts—choose thoughts that are positive and feel good; energize them and keep optimizing your emotions and how you feel.

"Think of at least 10 things that you love about yourself and fill your heart with joy."
Dr. Niva

Billion-Dollar Mind Journal Section

"When you better your best, your best has just gotten better."

RICK MACCI

Billion-Dollar Mind Journal Section

"Get rid of the negativity around you. Juice yourself with positive info and always talk in the mirror every day and say motivating things to the person looking at you."

RICK MACCI

Billion-Dollar Mind Journal Section

"What you think of yourself is more important than what your opponent thinks."

RICK MACCI

BILLION-DOLLAR MIND

"Every day, say to yourself powerful positive, motivating words, and you will be amazed it is better than any energy drink on the market."

- RICK MACCI

CHAPTER 8

Motor Mental Diet and Exercise: Positive Affirmations

Gaining a deeper understanding of basic neuroanatomy, we now recognize the involvement of sensory inputs, motor outputs, and the parasympathetic and sympathetic nervous systems in response to triggers like relaxation or stress. These systems interact with the mind, along with the persistence of ingrained thinking loops developed since childhood.

Summing up the key players of the mind: sensory inputs, motor outputs, parasympathetic and sympathetic nervous systems, and ingrained thinking loops.

Moving forward, let's explore methods to fortify our minds and regulate our thoughts, ultimately shaping them into resilient, billion-dollar assets. This journey encompasses a wide range of motor outputs and sensory inputs, with a paramount focus on positive affirmations.

What are Positive Affirmations?

Affirmation comes from the Latin origin, "affirmare" or to make firm. Positive affirmations are constructive statements that we encounter daily, serving as reminders of our forthcoming accomplishments. They introduce empowering ideas into both our conscious and subconscious minds, contributing to the strengthening of our mental faculties. Essentially, they act as sensory inputs, fostering a foundation for controlling our thoughts. By incorporating positive affirmations, we set in motion a chain of events where positive thoughts are generated, eventually manifesting into reality.

Why are Positive Affirmations Important for a Billion-Dollar Mind?

When we encounter a positive affirmation, we internalize and adopt it, leading to the formation of a positive thought. This positive thought then paves the way for a favorable outcome. Paula Whitman aptly describes positive affirmations as a "mental trampoline," offering us a mechanism to bounce back from stressful situations.[27] In moments of stress, we can focus on these affirmations, redirecting our thoughts toward positivity and subsequently enhancing the likelihood of a positive outcome.

Moreover, positive affirmations play a pivotal role in counteracting negative thoughts. These affirmations work to dismantle self-doubt and enhance self-confidence. By aligning our focus with the concept of winning and the positive outcomes we aim for, positive affirmations help us overcome self-imposed limitations and restrictive beliefs.

Maccisms

Rick Macci has a term called Maccisms which is a unique way of communicating with a positive tone to improve attitude and mental toughness. Maccisms are "all about the communication. When people read these Maccisms, such as: "A winner finds a way" or "Never make excuses" or "Keep popping the popcorn (keep moving your feet)" or "Extra butter (that means you've really got to move your feet)," they can relate to those things. More importantly, they remember them because they're catchy, unique and stick! And from Rick!"[28]

Personal Example of Positive Affirmations

During my early years as a tennis player, I maintained a consistent focus on the game, but I wasn't achieving the same level of success as my twin sister who excelled on the court. I often found myself facing losses and missing out on opportunities to participate in junior nationals, a stark contrast to my sister's achievements. Despite my love for the sport, I struggled to grasp the nuances of proper technique. Even with my mother's attempts to teach me, the mechanics of the forehand eluded me. I would gaze at the championship trophies held by those esteemed players from the Southern Tennis Association and silently wish I could taste victory myself. Yet, I would also doubt the possibility, thinking, "Winning seems so difficult." In my prayers, I sought guidance from a higher power, hoping for a path to victory that I couldn't see.

One fateful day, I acquired a copy of Paula Whittam's book, "Tennis Talk: Psych Yourself in to Win." Initially, I chuckled at the idea of positive affirmations altering my performance on the court. But during a lengthy plane journey to Southern California, curiosity got the best of me, and I decided to read it. As the sun streamed through the airplane window, illuminating the pages in my hand, I encountered lines like, "I remain calm and relaxed all match…I believe in myself" and "I always play to the best of my ability." I couldn't help but smirk inwardly, unconvinced that affirmations could transform my game. However, when I stepped onto the tennis court the following day, I noticed myself instinctively repeating these affirmations, particularly during high-pressure moments.

To my astonishment, my double faults decreased, and my forehand technique showed marked improvement. Throughout the match, I maintained the rhythm of positive affirmations and secured a victory. From that pivotal moment, I found myself drawn into the world of positive affirmations and the psychological aspect of the game. It was incredible to realize that a single positive thought held such incredible power and had the potential to propel me towards success.

I immersed myself in this newfound approach, combining my positive mindset with the technical knowledge I gained from my coaches. I treated tennis as a scholarly subject, meticulously documenting lessons, incorporating images, technical instructions, and winning strategies into my journal. This transformation led me to develop a winning streak, and I eventually achieved an undefeated status. Over multiple years, I earned the number one ranking in both Georgia and the Southern Tennis Association, surpassing even my twin sister's achievements.

Every morning, I dedicated at least 30 minutes to reciting positive affirmations, so much so that I ingrained within myself an unshakable belief in my assured victory even before stepping onto the court.

Positive affirmations help boost our self-image and can help retrain the mind to become more self-assured and confident. Affirmations can decrease stress and help individuals maximize their performance. Affirmations are a powerful way to train the brain to effectively cope with fears, failure, threats, and stress, resulting in optimal performance and confidence.

Olympic Gold Medal Discus Throw as a Result of Affirmations

Valarie Allman graduated from Stanford University and although she was already a champion, she wanted to raise her performance. She had won a silver medal, a bronze medal, and another silver medal but wanted to continue to win. She had focused on optimizing her nutrition, technical knowledge, and more practice, but what she discovered was the turning point in winning a gold medal was positive affirmations. She describes mental strength as an important aspect of her performance. She used the affirmation, "I am capable of winning. I deserve to win. I will win," repeating them over and over again like a mantra before her gold medal victory for the United States in the 2020 Olympics in Tokyo. [29] The affirmations eliminated any self-doubt and transformed her mental state to a strong personal belief of victory, which she aligned with.

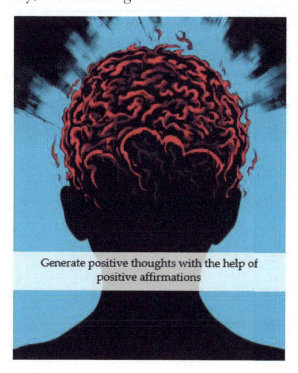

Generate positive thoughts with the help of positive affirmations

Positive Affirmations

Positive affirmations are a ladder for mental power,
Saying them can help you climb the highest tower.
Saying "I am the best,"
Will make you better than the rest.
One affirmation at a time,
Can support your highest climb.
Positive affirmations are the key,
To a life of positivity.
Give yourself the chance,
With positive affirmations, your mental power will enhance.

Billion-Dollar Mind Exercises

1. Incorporate positive affirmations into your routine.
2. Keep track of what you say to yourself and how many times. Positive self-talk is super important.
3. Say positive affirmations before going to sleep or upon waking in the morning.
4. Enhance positive affirmations' impact by pairing them with music to help embed them within your subconscious mind.
5. Display these affirmations on your phone, computer, sports bags, or any frequented spot to ensure consistent reinforcement.
6. Each positive affirmations should be encouraging, focus on the present moment, and view challenges as opportunities to grow. Think of a plan that will help you reach a certain goal, and keep the positive affirmations short, specific, authentic, and in the present tense. You can use these provided examples or customize your own:
   - I embrace myself, even in the face of mistakes, losses, or unmet goals.
   - I uplift and motivate myself.
   - I hold unwavering faith in my abilities.
   - I am a champion.
   - I am at ease with being at the top.
   - Just as nature creates beauty, I am a part of that beauty in every way.
   - I actively cultivate positive self-talk.
   - I dedicate myself fully each day.
   - I go the extra mile, transforming from ordinary to extraordinary.
   - I believe in myself.
   - I am a winner.

Billion-Dollar Mind Journal Section

"All greatness has to come from you and you alone."

RICK MACCI

Billion-Dollar Mind Journal Section

"See the big picture. Measure what's important by asking if it will be significant 10 years from now."

DR. NIVA

Billion-Dollar Mind Journal Section

"Think Big. Be Big."

RICK MACCI

Billion-Dollar Mind Journal Section

"Negative people get negative results."

RICK MACCI

"The most important thing in life is next. When you live in the past, you get passed."

- RICK MACCI

CHAPTER 9

Motor Mental Diet and Exercise: Letting Go of Past Memories

A crucial aspect of mind control involves managing our past memories. How can we cultivate positive, fulfilling, and successful thoughts if our minds are continuously replaying past events, particularly those that are negative or marked by failure? Thus, a fundamental strategy for mind control is to release the grip of the past, creating space for the emergence of new thoughts, memories, and achievements. These memories, often ingrained since childhood, maintain a profound influence on our actions as we mature, yet we often fail to recognize their deep-seated presence. "Letting" comes from old English and means to leave behind.

Consider memories from childhood—those that evoke fear, anxiety, or simply stand out. Those instilled with fear might hinder progress and success. For instance, a childhood encounter with a neighbor brandishing a gun could result in an irrational fear of others in adulthood. Similarly, the painful loss of a loved one to cancer might lead to a reflexive aversion to the word "cancer." Acknowledging these deeply rooted memories is pivotal, and releasing their hold enables healing and forward momentum. These personal memories, deeply embedded, can impact performance if left unaddressed.

Remarkable athletes, performers, and high achievers have mastered the art of swiftly releasing past mistakes. Top tennis players immediately let go of a missed shot or double fault to refocus on the next point.

A Parrot Who Freed Himself from His Cage

There was a story about a parrot who wanted to escape his cage and become free. One day he played dead and was quiet for some time. Because his master thought he was dead, the cage was opened. As soon as the cage opened, the parrot flew away and was free.

It is important to exercise this in our lives as this helps us let go of our past thoughts and sets us free. Imagine if you are looking back at your life as if it's already over and then figure out how you would minimize the small stuff and maximize what's important to you. This helps not only with perspective but also with letting go.

A Tennis Comeback

Jennifer Capriati is an American tennis prodigy who was the youngest tennis player to reach the top 10 in the world at age 14! Rick Macci trained her at age 10, one of his favorite students, knowing that she could be one of the best players in the world. Even when she was practicing against harder players as a young girl and got hit in the head by a ball, she continued to compete because she was able to let go and move on like a champion.

Jennifer was the youngest to reach semi-finals at the French Open, and to win a match at Wimbledon. She even won the gold medal at the Summer Olympics in Barcelona in 1992. She suffered personal setbacks including parental divorce. was caught up in shoplifting allegations, and was charged with marijuana possession.[30] Despite the personal setbacks, she managed to let go of her past and make a major comeback to become world number one in 2001. She used the ability to let go to come back stating: "I feel like I've started a new chapter in my life, and I need to leave the past behind."[31]

Letting Go: Keys For a Billion-Dollar Champion With a Billion-Dollar Mind

Roger Federer, the former men's number one tennis champion for 310 weeks and near billionaire, is known to have been very relaxed and positive during his career. He is present in every moment and is very natural with everything he does. He is very trusting and describes his personality as follows: "Maybe where my talent maybe has helped me a little bit is to shape and get the technique I have today that puts maybe less wear and tear on me...I think I've earned it by my schedule and my buildup, and maybe my mental side of the game as well. As much as I take things very seriously, I'm very laid-back, so I can really let go very quickly. This lunch, for example, is like a break for me. In my head, I'm able to say, 'Look, we just had a full-on practice and here I am actually able to relax and chill. And then we're going back to work again.' I think having that approach is really key."[32]

Letting Go

Letting go of the past sets you free,
There is no other true victory.
Let go of expectations and perfection,
And build your self-connection.
Let go of the past,
Or failure will come fast.
Letting go is the best feeling,
Love, happiness, and joy have no ceiling.
Try it and see,
Let go of your past and be free!

 ## Billion-Dollar Mind Exercises

1. Recall the ten most significant moments from your childhood. Reflect on these moments, document them in writing, and then assess their impact on your present life and thought processes. If you find that certain memories have yielded negative influences, make a conscious effort to release their hold.

2. When you encounter a memory from your past that holds pain, consider swapping it out for a more pleasant recollection or reimagine it in a way that aligns with your desired outcome. It's worth noting that these suggestions are not meant to replace professional medical assistance or guidance.

3. Release the tension and stress around the memory.

4. Imagine your thoughts as balloons, and if they are disturbing your peace of mind, let them go. Allow them to drift into the sky forever, never to return.

Billion-Dollar Mind Journal Section

"You've got to remember, but you also have to forget."

RICK MACCI

Billion-Dollar Mind Journal Section

"Letting Go of the Thought Patterns that do not serve you can change your world!"

DR. NIVA

Billion-Dollar Mind Journal Section

"Be like running water; let go, and everything will flow."

DR. NIVA

Billion-Dollar Mind Journal Section

"If you can train yourself with the skill to forget, that's how you're really going to have your peak performance. That's how you're going to be in the ideal performance state on a regular basis, and that's how you're going to play to the best of your ability on a regular basis. But that is one of the hardest things to do, having the ability to forget because it's right there in front of you. I like to take that even a step further with a lot of the players I coach."[33]

RICK MACCI

BILLION-DOLLAR MIND

"Make adversity your best friend. Having the ability to flip it in your mind and turn Mr. Negative into Mr. Positive is the key to unlocking any door to find your true potential."

- RICK MACCI

CHAPTER 10

Motor Mental Diet and Exercise: Flip it fast!

There are instances when we can easily manage simple sensory inputs. If a negative trigger arises, we can sidestep it. By infusing our minds with positive affirmations, constructive associations, and confident visualizations, we can exert control. Yet, at times, the world may seem to crumble around us. Unforeseen tragedies, natural calamities, terminal illnesses, or such challenges in competition, such as unjust advantages, injuries, and unanticipated environmental conditions can derail our progress.

During these challenging moments, the concept of "flipping it," as described by Rick Macci in his book, *Macci Magic*, becomes vital. Quickly transforming a negative event into a positive wellspring of mental energy can reshape the situation into a force for triumph.

Consider Michael Jordan's response when he faced a booing crowd. He channeled this negativity into playing better and achieving victory. Champions possess an inherent inclination to "flip it," as it beats succumbing to negativity and inevitable defeat. The capability to flip it is the cornerstone of cultivating a billion-dollar mindset. Speed is crucial. The faster the event is flipped, the quicker the mind is ready to move on and focus on winning.

Reframing

The origin of the word "frame" comes from old English and means to make a flick with the thumb; we are using the concept with our mind. "Flipping it" entails automatically reinterpreting a negative narrative into a positive one. Instead of telling yourself that you lost a match and are an inadequate tennis player, try affirming, "This loss offers me an opportunity to excel next time, to advance and elevate my skills." By reevaluating events, accepting the disappointing situation, and adopting a new perspective as fast as possible, you can make winning the desired outcome in every circumstance you face.

For example, the renowned tennis player Roger Federer embraced a windy playing condition by declaring, "Playing in the wind was an enjoyable challenge." As Rick Macci aptly puts it, view challenges as an essential part of the journey toward your next triumph. Negative situations can be transformed into positive ones today if you rewrite the script and initiate a positive shift right now. For instance, if you feel it's cold, then consider it an opportunity to experience something colder. If you are playing tennis in the sun, make the sun your best friend and even the wind, saying things to yourself such as, "I love the wind. The wind's my best friend. I'm smarter than the wind. I have better footwork in the wind. I play great in the wind." Flipping a situation not only makes a negative situation turn into a positive one, but also helps with enabling you to let go of the past and forget. Take a negative situation, make it a challenge, and flip it to a positive quickly to improve mental strength, intensity, and focus.

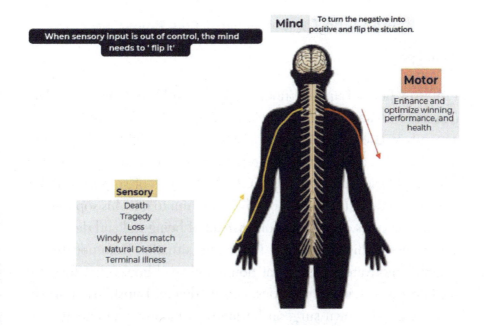

Winning a Tennis Match Despite a Parade

An anecdote from Rick Macci's experience during a tennis tournament exemplifies the power of flipping it to improve focus. Despite his opponent's racket-banging frustration and the parade lighting off fireworks, Macci maintained his unwavering focus, demonstrating his ability to control his mind and secure an easy victory. While the opponent was complaining about the noise, Rick said, "Right then there was no doubt in my mind that I would win this match simply because of my experience of being able to flip it saying, I loved the Willingboro marching band. I loved the fireworks. I never had so many friends on Harley-Davidsons in my life. I love all these M-80s, silver salutes, cherry bombs, lady fingers going off. I loved it. I embraced it. Because when it's all said and done, it is what it is. You have a choice."[34]

From Homebound Teen to World-Class Physician and Scientist[35]

Professor James Lupski, Cullen Professor and Vice Chair of molecular and human genetics at Baylor College of Medicine in Houston, grew up in Hicksville, N.Y. He and four (out of eight) siblings were found to have a hereditary neuropathy when they were born called Charcot Marie Tooth Disease (CMT). A series of surgeries on his feet and ankles after the age of 15 caused him to miss his sophomore and junior years of high school. Instead of being sad and depressed about missing high school, he flipped his situation from negative to positive, motivated to study at home and read books that fostered his interest in science, genetics, and medicine. Lupski used his resources and his own surgeon became his mentor and encouraged him to go into medicine. He used his medical degrees, research training, and his passion for the field to further the field of CMT, doing amazing research to identify the first gene to be associated with CMT, *PMP22*, which is responsible for approximately 70 percent of CMT cases. With continued Muscular Dystrophy Association support, Lupski's team identified a handful of other genes associated with CMT.

Flip It

Why does flipping a pancake seem easier than flipping a thought?
Flipping a negative thought can be a lot.
When things don't go our way,
It's easy to sway.
We want to blame it on everything around us,
But this can create a waste of energy and fuss.
So think how powerful it can be,
To go from negativity to positivity.
A negative thought makes things worse
So turning it into a positive can keep it from being a curse.
Flipping a negative thought can make you soar high,
Now your thoughts will take your positivity to the sky.

 ## Billion-Dollar Mind Exercises

1. Before you go to sleep each night, jot down a negative thought or unfavorable event that occurred during the day. Take the time to practice the art of flipping it—reframe it into a positive interpretation or envision a positive outcome.

2. When faced with stressful situations, pause and ask yourself, "Will this truly hold significance in a decade?" This perspective shift enables you to perceive each circumstance from a different angle.

3. Think of all the positives that happened with a certain event as the situation could have been worse.

4. Just like you jump rope or do repetitions in exercise, consistently flip negative thoughts or reframe thoughts so they are to your advantage.

5. Mentally time your ability to flip your thoughts so that the more you practice, the faster you can do this.

Billion-Dollar Mind Journal Section

"When you feed your brain positive food, everything will taste better."

RICK MACCI

Billion-Dollar Mind Journal Section

"Flip the script! You have the ability to turn every negative into a positive in your mind."

RICK MACCI

"Laughter, fun, and joy help the body relax. Having the ability to look at things in the exact opposite light of the way we're expected to look at it can mean the difference between extraordinary and ordinary."

- RICK MACCI

CHAPTER 11

Motor Mental Diet and Exercise: Humor to Improve Mental Health and Relaxation

What is Humor?

Humor helps people cope with environmental stimuli. Humor causes us to laugh and gives us amusement.

Humor's influence extends to productivity, creative thinking, and the cultivation of trust. It aids in adopting a broader perspective and embracing a light-hearted approach. Including humor in your sensory toolbox is a crucial step in elevating your mental resilience.

Engaging in enjoyable activities and wearing a smile can trigger feelings of serenity and vigor, thereby fostering an optimal state for both mental and physical performance. An example of this can be observed in the approach taken by tennis coach Rick Macci, who prioritizes creating an enjoyable environment for students at his academy.

Being fun and funny can increase dopamine, resulting in improved mood and motivation. If you are unable to smile, then life is becoming too serious. Smiling and laughter are easy and quick remedies that can help with stress and can improve our thoughts.

You've likely come across the saying that laughter is a potent remedy. This holds true. Laughter and humor possess the ability to alleviate mental stress, and their benefits extend to other aspects of health, including enhanced oxygen intake, reduced stress response, muscle relaxation, strengthened immune function, pain relief, and an improved mood. In essence, laughter can be likened to aerobic exercise. Its effects include a subsequent muscle relaxation response that can last for up to 45 minutes.

An Olympic Gymnast Uses Humor to Keep Her Going

Gabby Douglas is a U.S. Olympic gold medalist in gymnastics and in her book, "Grace, Gold, and Glory," she uses humor throughout her journey to keep her going.

At one point in her career, Gabby was away from her family and about to give up her gymnastics career when her mom surprised her, and she and her family stayed in a hotel for Christmas. Even without a tree or any amazing activity, she was with her family, laughing for days. They even had fun watching their mom in the hotel gym and Gabby had made her mom do impossible workouts. Gabby was laughing so much that it helped her homesickness and sadness. She then quoted her brother when he said, "If you want to be the best, you've got to take out the best," which was a turning point in her motivation.[36] She started to set goals and would visualize using vision boards to keep focused on her dreams. In addition to the laughter, she used positive affirmations to help her keep her mind strong to reach her goal. Her mom posted positive affirmations, a secret to success which she would say every day:

"I can do all things through the anointing, which strengthens me.

I am strong and I compete beautifully on vault, bars, beam, and floor.

My routines are amazing because the Greater One lives on the inside of me.

I refuse to give up! I refuse to quit! I push toward my dream, knowing that it will be my reality. I will achieve and be successful at everything I set my hand to do.

I am a winner. I am a fierce competitor. I am a phenomenal gymnast." [37]

On her rise to the top, she was able to handle flippant comments about her hairstyle, making a choice not to let it distract her. She never wasted even a second on negative thoughts. As a result of her mental strength and focus on positivity, she became the fourth American female gymnast to win gold amongst her many other accomplishments.

Humor

Joy can come from being funny,
Joy makes life so bright and sunny.
Laughing all day,
Can take negativity away.
Laughing brings out good thoughts,
That can't be purchase or bought.
Laugh and you'll see,
You'll start to feel incredibly.

 **Billion-Dollar Mind Exercises**

1. Set aside moments each day to indulge in laughter. Identify the sources of humor that resonate with you and ensure they are present during times of stress. Cultivate the habit of smiling, especially when faced with pressure.

2. Engage in 10 activities that infuse joy, laughter, and happiness into your life. Employ these activities as a means to redirect yourself from a negative mindset to a more positive state. Regardless of their scale or perceived significance, committing to activities that bring you happiness marks the initial stride towards cultivating positivity and a sense of well-being.

# Billion-Dollar Mind Journal Section

> *"Train your mind every day to be positive."*
>
> *Rick Macci*

# Billion-Dollar Mind Journal Section

> *"If my thoughts are in my control, then my joy is in my control."*
>
> DR. NIVA

Billion-Dollar Mind Journal Section

"With so much expectations and everybody thinking that they're the next big thing in tennis, I've always tried to be very serious about work that has to be done and taking ownership. But also in the way that I try to connect with players and motivate and inspire them I always want it to be fun. I always want to create passion in them. I want them to have that enjoyment, the love to play and looking forward to coming to practice, looking forward to training hard." [38]

RICK MACCI

_____
_____
_____
_____
_____
_____
_____
_____
_____
_____
_____
_____
_____
_____
_____

"The greatest ever in anything had the most positive attitude about everything. A positive attitude is available on your calendar 24/7, and you have an open invite. A bulletproof positive attitude and mindset is the cornerstone of handling the zigs and zags, and the good, the bad, and the ugly of every situation with which you deal. Winners find a way and losers make excuses."

- RICK MACCI

CHAPTER 12

Motor Mental Diet and Exercise: Positive Attitude

A positive attitude necessitates no inherent talent. Attitude is a CHOICE and is your response to specific events. Attitude derives from the Italian word, *attitudine*, which refers to disposition.

Possessing a positive attitude serves as the cornerstone of mental resilience. Attitude involves the disposition to react in a particular manner to given circumstances. Embracing positivity in every circumstance positions you to perceive the world from a distinct perspective. A positive attitude empowers you to exert maximum effort, establishing the foundation for any endeavor. With a positive attitude, you anticipate triumph instead of merely wishing for it.

Acknowledge your accountability for your thoughts and emotions. Shifting from negativity to positivity lies entirely within your control. A positive attitude directs attention to the favorable aspects of situations or challenges, anticipating favorable outcomes.

Attitude can be more important than knowledge. It is important to have a good attitude toward knowledge; what you do with the knowledge is more important than the knowledge itself. Having a positive attitude allows you to deal with situations in a confident and positive way.

Positive Attitude in a Concentration Camp

Viktor Frankl, a neurologist, was forced in the 1940s to join the Theresienstadt concentration camp where his father died of pneumonia and poor conditions. His mother and brother were murdered in gas chambers and his wife died of typhus.

Viktor survived these horrifying experiences, and he stated that despite being inflicted pain externally, "Everything can be taken from a man but one thing: the last of the human freedoms—to choose one's *attitude* in any given set of circumstances, to choose ones' own way."[39]

Man Born With Rare Physical Disability Uses a Positive Attitude by Shifting From "I can't" to "How can I?"[40]

Nick Santonastasso was born with Hanhart Syndrome, leaving him with no legs and just one arm. He has now become an inspirational speaker, author, bodybuilder, and model despite his physical limitations. He described his positive attitude in his book, "Victim to Victor".

As soon as he was born, his parents focused on the positive, like his beautiful head of hair and healthy organs. It was a miracle that he survived, and he was grateful for his life. Despite the challenges and obstacles, instead of saying "can't" he was taught to say, "how can I?" As a child, he struggled eating cheerios, but then discovered that he could lick his finger and pick them up with ease. He continued using a positive attitude and creativity to overcome his challenges: "it's important to stop worrying about people's opinions and to stop worrying about situations you have no power over, and to start focusing on things you do have power over. I always told myself, 'Okay, I need to do this. How can I approach it differently to get it done?' This was my attitude when I was growing up, and it's still my attitude today...Doing good for others can dramatically change your attitude about life. One of the good things I do in the world is work with a non-profit organization called New Beginnings Uganda. With the help of this organization, I was able to give money to a child in Uganda who broke his kneecap from his tibia to his fibula and didn't have money for the surgery he needed. He was going to lose a leg, but with the help of my small donation, his leg was saved. When I feel like crap, I remember this, and all of my negative mind chatter goes away." [41] He is so positive that he wants to train at Rick Macci's tennis academy to improve his serve!

Positive Attitude

A good attitude is a choice,
And a voice.
It must be sustained.
Despite tornadoes and hurricanes.
If you dig down deep in your heart,
It is what sets you apart.
Respond positively to an event,
And victory is imminent.

 ## Billion-Dollar Mind Exercises

Record in your journal how applying a positive attitude can enhance your circumstances. If you encounter a challenge, outline how adopting a positive attitude alone could aid in conquering it or altering your perspective. Reflect on the following instances:

- Generate positivity even in the face of defeat. Maintain a smile during trying moments. Cultivate a constructive vision for the future.
- Consistently uphold a positive demeanor in your thoughts, body language, and perspective. Respond positively to critiques or feedback.
- Assess your thoughts and eliminate all excuses, replacing them with optimistic solutions.

"For breakfast each morning have an 8 ounce glass of POSITIVITEA."
Rick Macci

Billion-Dollar Mind Journal Section

"If you want to be a true champion, start changing your attitude today."

RICK MACCI

Billion-Dollar Mind Journal Section

"If you have the physical capability, your attitude will determine everything. The best of the best don't make excuses. They always want to keep getting better. You can go through every sport and the best of the best are the most positive people and think differently! They keep training their mind as much as their body. It is about the wiring if you want to be the best you can be and extract greatness. Greatness looks over their shoulder so nobody sneaks up on them!"[42]

RICK MACCI

Billion-Dollar Mind Journal Section

"Players have 100% control over Attitude and Effort."

RICK MACCI

Billion-Dollar Mind Journal Section

"A positive attitude is more positive than any stroke."

RICK MACCI

"Gratitude is the number one energy drink everybody should have daily."

- RICK MACCI

CHAPTER 13

Motor Mental Diet and Exercise: Gratitude

Gratitude involves being appreciative and thankful, originating from the Latin word, *gratia*, which signifies gratefulness. It entails recognizing and valuing what you receive, contributing to an awareness of the positives in your life. Practicing gratitude enhances positivity and positively impacts health, relationships, and overall happiness. Gratitude plays a pivotal role in nurturing a billion-dollar mind, fostering optimistic thoughts, emotions, the enjoyment of positive experiences, improved well-being, resilience in the face of challenges, and the cultivation of meaningful relationships.

Gratitude and Improved Health

In a study conducted by psychologists, Dr. Robert Emmons and Dr. Michael E. McCullough, participants were divided into three groups: one group expressed gratitude, another criticism, and the third remained neutral. After 10 weeks, those practicing gratitude exhibited better health and a more optimistic outlook.[43]

Daily Gratitude for Those Who Teach You

Rick Macci recalls how Venus, Serena, and Richard Williams consistently expressed gratitude towards him and incorporated this practice into their routine. This technique is indispensable for enhancing mental strength and achieving success in life.

From Shark Bite Victim to Victorious Surfer

Imagine the scene: you're a young professional surfer, floating on your surfboard, chatting with your friend, when you are suddenly attacked by a shark. The traumatic event leaves you with only your right arm. Imagine losing not only your left arm but also your left arm and your career at 13 years old.

Bethany Hamilton experienced this tragic incident, but despite the tragedy, she returned to professional surfing. A key ingredient to her mental strength was her gratitude. When she rode a wave for the first time after the shark attack, she was incredibly thankful and happy inside. In her autobiography, she describes her spiritual faith and heartfelt appreciation for being alive. She feels that things could have been a lot worse and is so grateful for what she has. In 2005, Bethany won a national surfing title, and even inspired a movie based on her own story of overcoming obstacles. She is now an author, wife, and mother of three.

She quotes in her autobiography, "Soul Surfer: A True Story of Faith, Family and Fighting to Get Back on the Board": "I think it's for every person who is feeling down or defeated or a little lost in life, perhaps angry or frustrated by what's going on: For I know the plans I have for you,' declares the LORD, 'plans to prosper you and not to harm you, plans to give you hope and a future"…I think that if I can help other people find hope in God, then that is worth losing my arm for."[44]

Gratitude

Why should I say thank you?
They know I love them too.
Saying thank you and things as such,
Can be too much.
Why should I go overboard?
To say thank you to someone connected like a cord?
But when I realize that the connections don't know,
How much I truly appreciate them so,
I feel so happy,
To appreciate them so they can see.
That even if it's the millionth thank you,
It makes my heart and mind feel true.
Gratitude is better than money,
It feels so good and tastes sweeter than honey.
Make no mistake,
That sincere gratitude can't be faked.
Take it wherever you go,
And even without money, riches will flow.
It makes you mentally strong,
To appreciate everyone and everything that supports you along.

Billion-Dollar Mind Exercises

1. Each evening, before retiring for the night, compile a list of everything you are thankful for—no matter how simple—within a gratitude journal.

2. If there's someone you appreciate, mentally express your gratitude to them before going to sleep. Consider sending them a note through email or text message as well.

3. Incorporate daily gratitude practice into your routine.

Billion-Dollar Mind Journal Section

"When you practice gratitude, it will change your attitude."

RICK MACCI

Billion-Dollar Mind Journal Section

"As you look back on your life, reflect and be grateful for all the joyful moments you have had. Continue to build these joyful moments in the future."

DR. NIVA

Billion-Dollar Mind Journal Section

"The number one quality both Venus and Serena had as kids was not delivering daily fiesty attitude but delivering daily heartfelt gratitude."

RICK MACCI

"Confidence is magnetic and the most important thing you can teach a child. It should be taught everyday as an intangible vest that makes the vest more bullet proof."

— RICK MACCI

CHAPTER 14

Motor Mental Diet and Exercise: Self-Confidence

Self-confidence means trusting in your capacity to accomplish tasks despite challenges and embracing bold decision-making without hesitation.

Confidence comes from the Latin word, *confidere*, which means to have full trust. What's fascinating is that many people are more able to trust in others than in themselves! Lack of self-confidence is a major stumbling block for people's ability to live the life of their dreams.

Consider self-confidence as the flowing water in a house—it keeps things running smoothly, but its absence leads to significant consequences. Similarly, lacking confidence has substantial negative impacts. It shapes your perception of the feasibility of goals. It empowers you to take risks, explore new avenues, and step beyond your comfort zone. Confidence fuels the drive to become a frontrunner and make informed decisions.

Even if you don't currently feel confident in yourself, you can cultivate confidence through persistent repetition and practice and keeping your promises to others and to yourself. Giving up on a goal you set should be considered as breaking a promise to yourself. You would never make a commitment to someone you cared for, then break it, right? Make sure you have that same steadfastness when it comes to keeping commitments to yourself. This approach paves the way to attaining your objectives without succumbing to setbacks.

Self-confidence is a motor output. By projecting confidence, you foster positive thoughts that align with your goal of mastering thought control, eventually leading to productive, optimistic, and successful actions.

Believing in yourself and your ability to excel while recognizing attainable goals defines self-confidence—a paramount tool within our mental toolkit.

Confidence in the Face of Ridicule[45]

Edward Jenner was born in 1749 and he was fascinated with nature and science. He studied medicine but spent time experimenting with hydrogen balloons, as well as studying cuckoos and their offspring. He was elected as a fellow of the Royal Society of England even though many of his peers found him odd. He started to investigate how smallpox inoculation would protect from cowpox as well. He then became interested in deliberated forms of protection. Once he used cowpox lesions to inoculate an eight-year-old boy with cowpox, and there was a mild infection with no disease.

He sent his papers to the Royal Society with his observations but it was rejected! Undeterred, he privately published a book about "vaccinations" using the Latin word for cow, which is *Vacca*. Despite his publications, at first no one volunteered for vaccinations. Over time, other doctors started to support vaccinations and he started to send it to his medical acquaintances who requested it. Thomas Jefferson supported the cowpox vaccine in the United States. Despite being honored for his vaccine, Edward was attacked and ridiculed for his revolutionary idea. He had tremendous self-confidence to continue his activities on vaccination.

He was relentless and dedicated towards his goal with self-confidence to help change and save the world with his vaccine concept.

Instilling Confidence to Create Greatness

As young tennis students of Rick Macci, both Venus and Serena Williams felt that they were conditioned into believing they could become number 1 tennis players. He would compare them to tennis stars to motivate them and make them believe that if they could work hard, they could achieve greatness. This is a key component of how he builds excellent and world-class tennis players.

"Never let your own self-double stop you from living your dreams."

Dr. Niva

Self-Confidence

There is nothing more powerful than self-confidence,
It's like a protective fence.
Self-confidence allows you to achieve,
When no one else will believe.
It allows you to solve world mysteries,
And propels you to change history.
Self-confidence is a must,
You have to have self-trust.
All of life's puzzles have been this way,
With leaders who have had to pave the way.
They were alone with no outside support,
But self-confidence gave them a mental fort.
The greatest things in life were achieved,
With a strong self-belief.
So go forward, have confidence, and be bold,
And your mental strength and success will unfold.

 ## Billion-Dollar Mind Exercises

Alongside positive affirmations, these activities can bolster self-confidence:

1. What are your strengths? What comes easy to you? What makes you better than everyone else? When do you feel you are in a zone of maximal productivity, success, and fulfillment?

2. Record your top five accomplishments and contemplate the steps you took to accomplish them. Every morning, affirm to yourself, "I believe in myself." What obstacles did you overcome during the process? What makes you special to others? Recognize that even if you appreciate yourself, it is still less than what it truly is, so raise your evaluation of your personal greatness.

3. If you have lost confidence, write down everything that is going well for you rather than everything going against you. Mentally visualize the positive forces and the positive outcome of success. Always keep that mental picture of yourself.

4. If you feel inferior or self-doubt, why do you feel this way? Figure the way and eliminate the origin, which may have come from childhood experiences.

5. Identify any negative thought patterns or tendencies to compare yourself to others. When these thoughts arise, jot them down on paper and then discard the paper. Minimize the negative thoughts, obstacles or difficulties until they are eliminated.

Billion-Dollar Mind Journal Section

"When the world is against you, that is when greatness is discovered."

RICK MACCI

Billion-Dollar Mind Journal Section

"Confidence can hide the technical flaw. A Lack of confidence can find the flaw. No technical flaws become flawless."

RICK MACCI

Billion-Dollar Mind Journal Section

"Because let's face it, in life when people get confidence, they feel they can do anything. So building the big "C" in people is gigantic and that's been one of the springboards in my teaching and in these Maccisms that has triggered many people to not only go on to become some of the best players in the world but to be the best they can be. They've maxed out their ability because I get them to believe before they have any chance to think about believing."[46]

RICK MACCI

_____
_____
_____
_____
_____
_____
_____
_____
_____
_____
_____
_____
_____
_____
_____
_____
_____
_____

"When you love the grind, you will less likely get behind."

- RICK MACCI

CHAPTER 15

Motor Mental Diet and Exercise: Self-Discipline

Self-discipline is a crucial puzzle piece interconnected with self-confidence and self-motivation. It's derived from the word, discipline, which means instruction and training. As soon as you attain self-discipline through a positive achievement, your mind elevates to higher levels of self-love, positivity, and confidence. This enables your mind to generate even more positive thoughts and emotions. Acts of self-discipline breed positive thoughts as your mind recognizes its differentiation from others and senses deserving rewards due to earned self-discipline.

Self-discipline lends you **MENTAL** power so you can achieve the other things in your life. Discipline connects your present state with your dreams.

Self-discipline involves assuming full ownership of your life, being entirely responsible, and translating your plans into actions. It's the driving force behind achieving your goals. In the face of external distractions, self-discipline empowers you to maintain an unwavering focus on your objectives. Given its focus on goals and determination to achieve them despite external influences, challenging your mind with self-discipline tests is important. At the end of this chapter are challenges to assess your control over your mind.

Self-discipline is a no-excuse attitude, doing the things you do NOT love every day consistently. This is an important principle in self-discipline as we have to judge an activity based on a delayed reward, on how you feel once it's done, or once you've achieved your goal. Self-discipline needs to be worked on and, once achieved, it improves self-control, willpower, better performance, and improved mental control. It is important to be disciplined not one day but every day and continue to improve every day.

From Divorced, Depressed, and Impoverished Single Mom to Billionaire Author

J.K. Rowling is a famous author who has amassed billions through a billion-dollar mind technique of self-discipline. Having only been newly married, she took her baby daughter and escaped from an abusive and controlling spouse. She eventually returned to Edinburgh, Scotland where she wrote the renowned Harry Potter series.

She had no money, was receiving social security, and her living situation was bleak. 'The best you could say about the place was that it had a roof," she recalled.[47] "If I concentrated hard enough maybe I'd be able to block out the sounds of mice behind the skirting board."[48] She was depressed and miserable, once noticing that her baby daughter had such few toys compared to others. Every day, once her daughter was asleep, Rowling would put her baby in the stroller and walk half an hour to a café called Nicholson's to write her book. Through self-discipline, she would write with one hand while rocking her baby with the other. She had to escape an unheated apartment as well as find a place for her to drink coffee while she wrote. She describes a catch-22 trap for impoverished single parents—to get jobs and earn money for daycare, they need daycare. Despite these struggles, she submitted her book to 12 publishers who turned it down until someone finally agreed to take a chance on her work. Despite countless obstacles, her mental self-discipline led her to be named Woman of the Year and she is now one of the most celebrated and richest women in the world.

Self-Discipline

We hear the word self-discipline,
And think, oh not again!
It's the 3,000th daily jump rope,
Which initially can give us a loss of hope.
But if you recognize that every little action,
Can give you massive attraction.
You will now see,
That jumping 3,001 times is a victory.

 ### Billion-Dollar Mind Exercises

Document your goals and outline the steps of discipline required to attain them. Keep track of these goals daily within a journal and take responsibility for adhering to the actions necessary to achieve them.

"Never give up! A 1% improvement matters and makes a new and better version of you every day."
Dr. Niva

Billion-Dollar Mind Mental Challenges

Is your mind conquered self-discipline and under your control? Gauge yourself with these mental challenges:

1. Consume less food than you typically would to feel 100% full. Date achieved:
2. Take a small bite of dessert and save the remainder for later or abstain from eating it altogether. Date achieved:
3. Consume a new nutritious food item for 14 days. Date achieved:
4. Perform one additional repetition of an exercise at the gym after your regular set. Date achieved:
5. Engage in something you fear. Date achieved:
6. Undertake something you harbor self-doubt about. Date achieved:
7. Cultivate a positive thought about something or someone you usually dislike. Date achieved:
8. Take a deep breath when angry and maintain your composure. Date achieved:
9. Learn something new every day. Dates achieved:
10. Stretch or perform a few exercises while waiting in a long line. Date achieved:
11. Practice amid loud distractions, unfavorable conditions, and opponents who cheat. Date achieved:
12. Respond with a smile rather than reacting when you feel insulted. Date achieved:

13. Forgive yourself for a mistake. Date achieved:

14. Listen fully to comprehend the complete story before reacting. Date achieved:

15. Refrain from judging someone based on appearances. Date achieved:

16. Persevere even when faced with rejection. Date achieved:

17. Embrace competition regardless of the circumstances. Date achieved:

18. Receive criticism with enthusiasm for the sake of improvement. Date achieved:

19. Take a calculated risk to propel you towards your goal. Date achieved:

20. Identify a constraining thought, eliminate it, and replace it with an empowering one. Date achieved:

21. Assume command of your life by preparing your clothes, bags, or goals for the next day the night before. Date achieved:

Billion-Dollar Mind Journal Section

"To get the real edge, practice on your day off."

RICK MACCI

Billion-Dollar Mind Journal Section

"When you get up early and master boring, the competition is still asleep mastering snoring."

RICK MACCI

Billion-Dollar Mind Journal Section

"If you stay after practice and hit serves, your mind gets better than your serve."

RICK MACCI

Billion-Dollar Mind Journal Section

> "Tennis and life are similar: great preparation leads to a great result."
>
> RICK MACCI

"When you fail, miss, or lose, always look at it as a tremendous, exciting great opportunity to find a better way. This is a champion's mindset."

- RICK MACCI

CHAPTER 16

Motor Mental Diet and Exercise: Self-Improvement

What is Self-Improvement?

Self-improvement is a crucial element in our journey to achieve our goals. The word improvement comes from an Anglo-French origin to empower, which mean to turn into profit. Properly embraced, self-improvement can foster a sense of deserving victory and reward. However, it's important to approach self-improvement carefully, as it can become a double-edged sword. If taken to an extreme, it might lead to negativity, critical thoughts, depression, and an overreaction to external feedback.

Yet, viewing self-improvement as an exciting opportunity for growth is the right perspective. It's a chance to elevate ourselves and acquire new skills.

Why is Self-Improvement Important to a Billion-Dollar Mind?

Another important aspect of self-improvement is that it helps our minds and thoughts focus on ourselves rather than scrutinize other people. We look inward at fixing ourselves rather than fixing or criticizing others. This perspective helps us focus on a bigger picture of self-improvement rather than worrying about insignificant minutiae.

Self-improvement contributes to effective mind control by enabling us to tap into our maximum potential, striving for excellence. When handled correctly, it becomes a catalyst for cultivating positive thoughts and achieving success, while also bolstering self-confidence and self-discipline.

Negative perceptions of self-improvement can hinder personal growth and progress.

Often, self-improvement arises from facing rejection. Although rejection can be painful, it's important to recognize that facing rejection or failure is far superior to inaction. In essence, facing challenges and learning from them, whether they result in failure or success, can lead to more favorable outcomes than not taking any action at all.

Self-improvement is a delicate process that should be done gradually and carefully. Striving for too much too soon can overwhelm the mind, potentially causing your thoughts to spiral downward into a negative state, resulting in depression. It's a very helpful component but, if not approached with care, can have negative repercussions.

It is important not to be attached to the results for self-improvement and not to take self improvement personally.

Failure has been linked to physical danger for early humans, and our minds have been programmed that rejection is scary and should be avoided to survive and avoid pain. But if we work on exposing ourselves to repeated rejections and failures, we can eliminate this fear of hearing no and the fear of being rejected in order to have the self-confidence to ask for anything.

Too much negative feedback can result in negative self image or depression

Too little feedback can result in lack of self improvement

Self improvement ca be a double edged sword. Solution: Take feedback and self improvement in small amounts and doses that you can personally handle and keep increasing it until you develop an ability to handle almost any feedback that comes your way.

British Cyclists Improved Their Pillows and Mattresses to Win! [49]

Back in 2003, the British Cycling team wasn't achieving very much until they brought Dave Brailsford on as the director. Brailsford focused on making incremental improvements that together would lead to significant overall improvement. He concentrated on making 1% adjustments and marginal gains, beginning with comfortable bike seats, followed by the application of alcohol on the tires for better grip, heated shorts for ideal muscle temperature, more aerodynamic racing suits, the best massage gels to help with recovery, and the best pillow and mattress to sleep at night. After 5 years, they started to win gold medals, ultimately setting Olympic and world records. Through small but steady improvements over time, they achieved greatness.

A Tennis Champion Overcoming Sickness to Become the Greatest of All Time With Optimal Resilience [50]

Novak Djokovic is a champion athlete and tennis player, one of the greatest tennis players of all time. He currently is ranked as the number one men's tennis player in 2023, and has been ranked number one at the end of the year seven times. He has won multiple tennis titles including 24 Grand Slam titles at the time this book was written. He exemplifies resilience in this example as he conquered multiple thinking loop traps to reach his goal and become one of the best.

Before his first tennis lesson at age six, Djokovic knew he wanted to be a champion. He even packed his own tennis bag meticulously with a racquet, water bottle, rolled-up towel, extra towel, and wristbands, all neatly folded inside. He was called the golden child and for the following 17 years dedicated every day of his life to tennis.

But he started exhibiting signs of a concerning health issue while he was playing on the court. He suffered stomach pains and nausea, but couldn't figure out what was causing it. To improve his mental strength, he tried meditation and yoga, and even relocated to Abu Dhabi. However, it was the day he altered his diet that truly changed his life. He discovered that he had a gluten intolerance, and his parents owned a pizza parlor!

His dedication and discipline to create the best diet in the world made him even more extraordinary. He maintained a strict new diet, regimen, and control over his mental and physical well-being. He followed the same daily routine to maintain his health and fitness. Every morning he drank water, did yoga, ate breakfast, and practiced with his training partner. Afterwards, he would drink warm water and a sports drink filled with vitamins, minerals, and electrolytes. Then it was time for his sports massage before eating lunch. Once he finished eating lunch, he would lift weights and replenish his body with a pea protein drink, stretch once more, and then, for dinner, eat a high protein salad with no carbohydrates and no dessert. At night he would read, meditate, and write in his diary before falling asleep. He was so disciplined that after winning one of the longest matches in history, the 2012 Australian Open, he gave himself a tiny square of chocolate to taste.

He credits his war-torn past in Serbia for his open-mindedness and focus on the important things in life such as love. Novak Djokovic's excellent book, "Serve to Win" describes that he can eat honey, muesli, almond milk, fruits, nuts, chicken, fish, quinoa and water throughout the day avoiding lactose and gluten. Rick Macci also follows a similar gluten-free and lactose-free diet, consisting of chicken, salad, fruit, and nut bars. Rick includes popcorn, Gatorade, and yogurt, and this simple consistent daily diet for the past 20 years makes him feel energetic and great. Dr. Niva's diet consists of salad, protein, fruit, vegetables, oats, and nuts.

As we reflect on Novak's incredible story, we can imagine all of the countless thinking traps that could have entered his mind: he's from a war-torn country and doesn't have the resources to win; his gluten intolerance is incurable; he is a failure for not winning; Abu Dhabi was a waste of time; meditation didn't work; he will never succeed in his life. The list could go on and on. But what made him great was his ability to recognize these traps and overcome them. He was flexible, resilient to challenges, open-minded, and determined to learn more about nutrition in order to transform his life. Once he did this, he was committed to stick to it!

Djokovic Meditation Practice [51]

Djokovic describes how he meditates and keeps it simple. He will sit quietly, focus on his breathing, and then observe his thoughts as well as the physical sensations he is feeling. The thoughts flood his mind, but it's important to let them come and go as the physical sensations are real, but the thoughts are not.

It is quite impressive to read how Djokovic describes the awareness of his mental trap of negativity in his book, "Serve to Win" : "For me, I realized just how much negative energy I have coursing through my brain. Once I focused on taking a step back and looking at my thoughts objectively, I saw it plainly: a massive amount of negative emotion. Self-doubt. Anger. Worries about my life, my family. Fears about not being good enough. That my training is wrong. That my approach to a coming match is wrong. That I'm wasting time, wasting potential. After practicing meditation for a while, something clicked: This is simply how my mind works. It's probably how everyone's mind works. I wasted a lot of energy and time on my own 'inner turmoil,' or however you want to describe it. I was so focused on this inner battle that I lost sight of what was happening around me, what was going on in the moment. I've done so much mindful meditation that now my brain functions better automatically." [52]

Silence of the mind done through meditation or quiet inner reflection is a critical component of mental strength. The more silent we are, the more power we have when we do speak. Silence allows the unnecessary internal and external noise to be quieted.

From High School Basketball Reject to Billion-Dollar Basketball Star with a Billion-Dollar Mind[53]

Michael Jordan is one of the most legendary basketball players in the history of sport. He grew up in North Carolina and he would often lose to his older brother. When he was in high school, Jordan did not make the high school varsity team. He was devastated and cried after he didn't make the team. The loss made him so motivated that he worked extremely hard, practicing every day. His work ethic was unparalleled, pushing him to run so much that he was able to score more than 40 points each game. He finally got the call to be on the varsity team.

He started to become a phenomenal basketball player after having a setback in college because of his intense work ethic and ability to improve himself every day. He states, "I've missed over 9000 shots in my career, I've lost almost 300 games. 26 times I've been trusted to take the game's winning shot and missed. I've failed over & over & over again in my life. And that is why I succeed." [54]

Harder Conditions on the Tennis Court led to Stronger Court Performance for Two Legendary Tennis Champions

Venus and Serena Williams would practice with broken glass, old balls, and cheaters to help with their mental fitness. To enhance their skills, they even practiced with men. The sisters were willing to lose points during practice if it meant getting better in the long run. As Rick Macci describes them, they were so "over the Top determined, they would dart over broken glass to get a ball and dart back over it again to get the next one! Maybe that is why they ended on the Top!"[55]

Focusing on Improvement Rather Than Failures Led to the Design of a Legendary Cartoon Mouse [56]

Walt Disney is an American animator, entrepreneur, and film producer who created the famous Mickey Mouse. His famous creations, animations, and multiple Academy awards did not reach success without improvement.

For example, when he was creating short films, his first two failed, but his third film was a success because he worked hard to add a musical score and sound effects, setting a new standard for Disney productions forever.

Self-Improvement

When I hear self-improvement,
My heart sinks.
On no, what do they think?!
But when I look it as an opportunity,
To be the best I can be,
It is now the key,
To be the best version of me.
Feedback is a mirror of truth,
Better than a picture booth.
Give me more,
So to greatness I can soar!

 ## Billion-Dollar Mind Exercises

1. Begin by jotting down your goals, and then brainstorm ways in which you can enhance yourself to attain them. Visualize the ideal version of yourself and identify the key areas that need improvement to align with these goals. Envision the successful realization of your goals and chart out the positive thoughts and actions that will guide you on that journey.

2. Embrace the concept of failure and rejection as integral parts of self-improvement. The more you become at ease with these experiences, the greater your potential for growth and success. By cultivating comfort with rejection and failure, you increase your opportunities for achievement, ensuring you take action rather than being held back by discomfort.

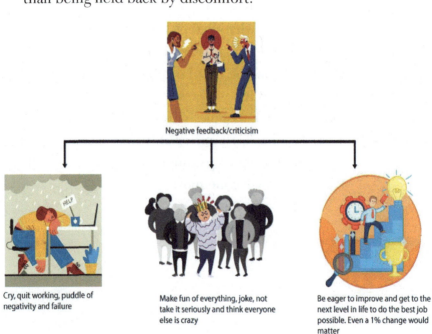

Billion-Dollar Mind Journal Section

"Rule number one, today get better. Rule number two, today: see rule number one."

RICK MACCI

Billion-Dollar Mind Journal Section

"Remember the best of the best failed so much, this is why they succeed!"

RICK MACCI

Billion-Dollar Mind Journal Section

"If you make a mistake and you don't correct it, you just made another one."

RICK MACCI

"When you have goals, you will score more goals."

-RICK MACCI

CHAPTER 17

Motor Mental Diet and Exercise: Focus

Concentration and focus involve directing your attention towards a singular objective at the right moment. This is crucial because when we center our focus on a specific goal, our thoughts naturally align with that goal. For instance, by repeatedly affirming "I am a winner" during a match or in our daily lives, we cultivate thoughts of triumph and channel our attention towards achieving victory. Various techniques aid in concentration and focus, such as establishing routines or rituals that guide our thought patterns towards winning. In the context of tennis, these might include bouncing the ball thrice before serving or maintaining a positive demeanor even after losing a point. Incorporating practices like stretching, pre-match visualization, or grounding exercises can also bolster focus.

To focus is to be in flow. To reach this state, work must be challenging, meaningful, and free of distracting feedback.

Non-Judgmental

The concept of nonjudgment complements the theme of mind control. When we engage in judging others, our focus on our goals and ourselves tends to erode. Passing judgments not only squanders time and energy but also hinders our concentration. Furthermore, it distracts us from our own pursuits. It's important to remember that complete understanding of someone else's circumstances is often elusive. Those who may appear frustrated, upset, or unusual may be dealing with personal trials, such as recent loss, terminal illness, or severe stress. Practicing nonjudgment contributes to enhanced concentration, improved focus, and a sense of inner peace. By abstaining from judging others, we maintain mental clarity and a healthy state of mind. This is reinforced by a quote from the book "power of thoughts": To become the master of your mind, you must desist from fault-finding, no matter how pleasant it seems.[57]

A Young Girl Travels from Russia to America, Focused on Becoming Number One [58]

Maria Sharapova, a former world's number 1 tennis player, came to America with her dad and almost no money. Through multiple struggles with tennis academies, coaches, and at times no place to stay, she and her dad focused on the goal of her becoming the number one tennis player in the world. While other girls were staying out late, she would be sleeping. She would sleep early, practice longer than others, and was on a mission to become number one. Other kids would eat candy, laugh, gossip, and some were rich and spoiled. She noticed that she was different and focused. She didn't worry about friends, her clothes, or her hair, because she was on the court focused and playing tennis to win. As she described in her autobiography and "Unstoppable: My Life so Far" what stood out to be the most remarkable aspect about her to Rick Macci when he coached her was her intense focus: "The best parts of my game, those things that made me hard to beat, were mental. They were my intensity, my focus. I could stay after my opponent shot after shot, game after game, never fading, never losing hope, even when I was behind."[59]

Coming from a Low-Income, Dangerous City to Winning 23 Grand Slams: a Tennis Champion with Unstoppable Focus[60]

Serena and Venus Williams grew up in the low-income housing projects of Compton, California. The area was known for crime, drugs, and violence. The sisters played on tennis courts littered with cracks, soda cans, beer bottles, fast food wrappers, and drug paraphernalia including syringes, tubes, and plastic bags. They even played while gunshots echoed in the streets. Their daddy would tell them to focus, play and not dwell on the negative.

Serena recounts in her autobiography, Serena Williams, My Life, "tennis was always there, like breathing." Going after the oldest, flattest tennis balls would be challenging but help with her concentration and focus. [61]

To improve focus, Serena's dad would place affirmations on the court: "If you fail to plan, you plan to fail." "Believe," " You are a winner." "Be humble." "Say thank you." "Focus." [62] Her parents would tell her to visualize everything in her head because whatever she and her sister wanted to become they would have to visualize it first.

When Serena and her family drove from California to Florida to train with Rick Macci, Serena noticed it was the longest stretch of time that they didn't play tennis! They were still so focused that at every rest stop they would swing their rackets while doing running and fitness exercises. In Florida, they were not only focused on conditioning and fitness training but also practicing with boys as arranged by Rick Macci; hitting with boys only made Serena more focused because the guys never let up, and she would lose badly at times. Despite the intense focus, Serena never felt pressured by her family. She describes another key to mental strength was that the focus wasn't about winning matches but more about improving: " If we could figure out a way to improve and win, so much the better."[63]

She focused on the court and off the court with her journal writing. "Writing can be an extremely effective tool for harnessing your energies and keeping your focus…it helped me to organize my thoughts and keep my objective in mind. It helped me to focus. Plus, there is great power in introspection, don't you think? And what better way to turn your thoughts inward and force yourself to reflect on your day, your goals, and your blessings than to stare at a blank page and reach for some way to fill in?"[64] Through her unwavering focus, she and her family were able to break through the financial and racial barriers, leading her to become one of the greatest tennis players ever, amassing a total of 23 Grand Slam titles.

Focus

Why should we focus?
It seems like hocus pocus!
There are phones, TVs, social media and fabulous fun,
endless distractions!
Why focus?!
With a million options to change our locus.
Without a doubt,
Your mind will shout,
"There's an overload!"
And it wants to explode!
So focus on your goal and task at hand,
It will keep you on top of slippery sand.
Focus is a mental power laser beam,
That can help you achieve your dream.
Don't let anything distract,
From all the achievements you can attract.
Focus is a super-power,
That will enhance every hour!

 **Billion-Dollar Mind Exercises**

1. Keep a daily journal, writing your thoughts, goals, and whether you have taken steps to achieve those goals as well as any obstacles you may have.

2. Craft a powerful affirmation consisting of 1-3 words that you can repetitively say to enhance your focus and cultivate a mindset of positivity and triumph.

3. Formulate a specific ritual that primes you for success.

4. Find a quiet space where you can sit undisturbed and assume the role of a silent observer of your thoughts. Recognize that the thoughts emerging are transient and not definitive. Let go of each thought as if releasing a balloon into the sky. Take deep breaths and anchor your attention to the present moment.

   Continue this process until your thoughts are clear and your mind attains a state of calm. A tranquil mind possesses the ability to perceive truths and concentrate effectively.

5. From this calm foundation, generate positive thoughts that are aligned with your desired goals.

Billion-Dollar Mind Journal Section

"Emotions can get int the Way or you train the brain to say No Way to get on your Way to GOAT STATUS."

RICK MACCI

Billion-Dollar Mind Journal Section

"When you do one more, just ONE more, those people seem to have WON more."

RICK MACCI

Billion-Dollar Mind Journal Section

"Concentration is having the maintenance man blowing off the sidewalk and you didn't hear him."

RICK MACCI

"Every day challenge your limits and do not limit your challenges and you will challenge others and not feel limited."

-RICK MACCI

CHAPTER 18

Motor Mental Diet and Exercise: Self-Motivation

Motivation is the driving force behind our personal goals and ambitions, fueling us with enthusiasm, energy, and purpose. It's a wellspring of potential energy that arises from the joy and passion for our pursuits. Once we've defined our goals, motivation can be cultivated towards achieving them. A crucial question in the process of generating motivation is asking ourselves, "Why?" After setting our goals, delving into why these goals hold significance for us is essential. While external influences can be positive, our internal well of motivation is what truly propels us forward, especially during challenging times.

Motivation comes from the Latin word, *movere*, which means to move. Motivation is the force of inspiration and enthusiasm that allows you to move toward your goal. The absence of motivation and exposure to unmotivated individuals can be contagious. In the eyes of young adults, being nonchalant or unenthusiastic might be considered "cool" or "popular," which can hinder the drive to excel or reach one's full potential. Substantial stressors like financial concerns, a history of setbacks, or difficulty handling pressure can also impede motivation. Many accomplished athletes, who excel under pressure, often associate themselves with other driven peers, and this mutual motivation aids them in performing at their peak.

How does motivation factor into the billion-dollar mind toolkit? By nurturing our internal well of energy and enthusiasm, we rely less on external sources for motivation. This internal motivation becomes a catalyst for action, which in turn generates the positive thoughts necessary to fuel our journey. We also expect to succeed and carry out the thoughts and actions that will get us there.

Motivation is increased when individuals come from a background of hardship and a tough life. They typically have had many struggles and were considered the underdogs. They don't want to go back so they continue to fight with a strong commitment to win.

From Slum Dwelling to Chess Champion[65]

Imagine living in a slum in Katwe, Uganda just trying to survive with no school, no father, selling maize on the street, and doing all the work—cooking, cleaning, and chores? Multiple floods and streams of raw sewage ran through the trenches bringing with them swarms of flies and a nauseating stench. There was no sanitation, electricity, or running water. There was only a cycle of misery of children raising children in utter poverty. Phiona Mutesi was born into such a life.

At age 9, she discovered playing chess could get her free food. Although she initially started playing for the food, she realized her hidden talent. Because she had a goal to get her family out of poverty and into a house, and a goal to become a grandmaster, she was *hungry* and *motivated*. That hunger and motivation helped her achieve her goals so that even when she had no money, no school, and no home, she was still committed to playing chess.

Phiona had a fierce competitive mindset and was very courageous. She would even walk five kilometers to get to the training center for chess. Despite never having read a chess book, magazine, or even used a computer, she became a national chess champion due to her drive and motivation. She devoted countless hours to the game, far more than any of the other children did. It was impossible to keep track of all the games Phiona played. She was not only good at understanding chess, but played as if her life depended on it—which, in many ways, it did.

A Boxing Legend Who Never Told Her Parents She Was Boxing[66]

Born in a village in Manipur, India, Mangte Chungneijang Mary Kom learned to work hard at an early age. She worked in the fields ploughing, handling heavy farm tools, and carrying rice sack bundles for planting and straw to store as cattle feed. She also had to haul water across long distances and collect firewood and fish. She cooked, washed clothes, gardened, cleaned, and did odd jobs around the house. Both her parents were landless farmers, so there was little money to feed and educate her and her two siblings. She learned an important life lesson: "what I sow, I will reap."

Mary Kom became passionate about boxing and found a coach on her own without telling her parents. She met her coach at a training center and paid for the admission, gloves, and guards all on her own. Her first pair of gloves were 350 rupees. She was unable to train with proper equipment as it was expensive. The young boxing hopeful couldn't even afford comfortable shoes. Even when she competed at nationals, her shoes were torn, but it didn't stop her or bother her. When she won her first gold medal, it was reported in a local newspaper and her father found out about it by chance by overhearing other men who were talking about it! Although her dad refused to let her box due to his fear of the potential injuries and risks involved, she refused to give up on her dream. Mary Kom convinced her parents to allow her to keep boxing and she continued saving money so she could excel in her athletic career. When she earned her first monetary reward, she used it to purchase a farm for her parents.

Mary Kom was committed, determined and motivated, becoming the only female World Amateur Boxing champion for a record six times. She has made history as the only female boxer to win a medal in seven World Championships, and the only female or male boxer to win eight World Championship medals. She has been ranked as the world's number one woman light-flyweight by AIBA as well as the first Indian female boxer to win a gold medal in the Asian Games in 2014 and at the 2018 Commonwealth Games. She is a record holder of being a six-time Asian Amateur Boxing Champion. "I do not rely only on my technique or strength but also my mind." "People used to say that boxing is for men and not for women and I thought I will show them some day. I promised myself and I proved myself." I had no support, no opportunity, no sponsors backing me for most of my career."[67] Mary Kom has admitted that dealing with very high degree of pressure becomes a part and parcel of the game. Pressure is inevitable and draws upon her mental strength to manage it. This is the same message that Rick Macci teaches that pressure should be your best friend.

She has also set up a boxing academy in her hometown, Imphal, and she and her husband take care of this academy together. If you ever feel lost or depleted in life, remember there is someone like Mary Kom who did not give up! "Hardships she faced in her youth were the foundation of her strength."[68]

Motivation

Why should we work hard and be number one?
When being lazy can be so fun?
When we realize we each have amazing unique talent,
Then the hours become precious and can't be lazily spent.
Don't be too late,
To recognize that improving the world was our fate.
So find out ways to self motivate,
At the earliest possible date.
In order for you to reach the stars,
Self motivation will make the journey seem less far.

Billion-Dollar Mind Exercises

1. Jot down your top five goals, and beneath each goal, articulate the reasons driving your desire to achieve them. Focus on improving your strengths and find your purpose.

2. Connect with fellow motivated individuals, including athletes.

3. Embrace and relish moments of pressure.

4. Keep track of your daily achievements and victories.

5. Ask yourself "why" you are doing something up to five times and figure out your true motivation and desire for a goal. Keep that *why* with you when you face difficulties.

Billion-Dollar Mind Journal Section

"Will defeats skills always."

RICK MACCI

Billion-Dollar Mind Journal Section

"Greatness Time and Time again is doing what nobody even thinks of Around the Clock to get the edge every Day every Hour every Minute every Second."

RICK MACCI

Billion-Dollar Mind Journal Section

"The Drive for Success comes from Within."

DR. NIVA

Billion-Dollar Mind Journal Section

"Williams sisters. I just knew because of how big they were going to be and how fast. The women's game had never seen it. If they could just get those strokes, they had those key elements. I knew they had that hunger because they wanted to succeed because they had nothing. They had that drive to want to do it. We were on a mission and they had athleticism that the sport hadn't seen yet. Size, speed and power. They were competitors first and tennis players second. That is the real key! But technically they were still a train wreck. Just a lot of things were really way off. They hadn't had world-class instruction. But the way they competed, and they didn't want to lose the point, to me their stock rose even more. To me that's always the X factor, the way someone competes. Venus and Serena had a deep down burning desire to fight and compete at this age. It was unique. Unreal hunger." [69]

RICK MACCI

_____
_____
_____
_____
_____
_____
_____
_____

BILLION-DOLLAR MIND

"The most important thing you do is right now. Think like that and your focus and energy will grow every day. Changing your mind is much better than changing the channel. The difference between great and good is the microscopic, invisible, inner, intangible of the mind."

- Rick Macci

CONCLUSION

The mind is a tool that can work for or against us. As we wrap up this book, consider the mind as a game in which we contend with our own true selves. The central idea of this book is to equip you with the tools to triumph in the battle against your own mind and claim victory over it.

Initially, embarking on a journey through your own mental landscape is crucial to comprehend your mental patterns. Armed with this understanding, you'll engage in a winning match—you against your own mind. We challenge you today to take these concepts and use them in your life so that you can think of your desired thoughts and create the life you deserve.

The only person limiting your thoughts is YOU. So, believe in yourself and take a step forward toward your goals just by changing one thought at a time. We went on a journey through the sensory, motor, and autonomic nervous systems. The sensory system involves different sensory inputs to our mind including our five senses, positive thoughts, positive associations, visualization, and self-love. The motor system involves feeding our mind with acts of positive affirmations, letting go, flipping it, humor, positive attitude, gratitude, self-confidence, self-discipline, self-improvement, focus, and self-motivation. The autonomic nervous system involves the parasympathetic and sympathetic components, which endorses smiling and deep breathing to balance the sympathetic and parasympathetic systems for an ideal performance state. Each of these components fits and enhances the others like perfect puzzle pieces. For example, humor can help with letting go, which can help with positive thoughts, focus, and self-love. As Rick Macci says, if you can implement even ONE of these chapters into your daily life, you have WON! So don't delay and start working on your mindset right away.

As we conclude this book written with love and a desire to improve your world, don't forget to add a smile to your day, breathe deeply, and say positive things to yourself and you will become stronger than you know! Remember that by controlling the input your senses receive and consistently feeding your mind with positive, joyful, and successful thoughts, you can achieve your desired outcomes. This approach forms a protective mental sphere, enabling you to cultivate an unwavering, resolute mind.

"Every action and emotion in life is started by a thought. Take care of your thoughts as you would take care of a garden to create the life your desire."

Dr. Niva

Billion-Dollar Mind Visual Summary

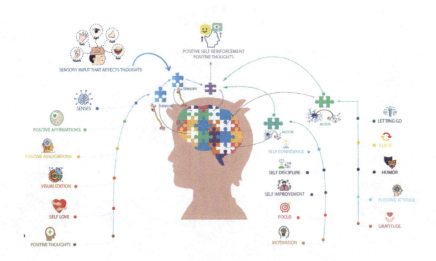

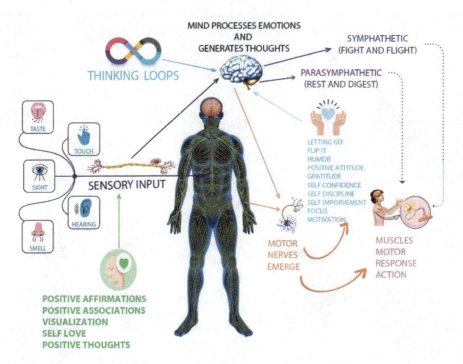

Billion-Dollar Mind Journal Section

"Remember the best of the best failed so much, this is why they succeed!"

RICK MACCI

Billion-Dollar Mind Journal Section

"The mind is either for your or against you. Make a choice."

RICK MACCI

Billion-Dollar Mind Journal Section

"The mind is the ultimate weapon. Make sure you don't use it on yourself."

RICK MACCI

ABOUT THE AUTHORS

In 1991, the world-renowned and legendary tennis coach, Rick Macci, was poised to revolutionize the realm of tennis. That year marked a pivotal moment when he took an audacious step: he ventured to Compton, California, to meet two yet-to-be-famous sisters, Venus and Serena Williams. Despite the risks, Macci recognized their immense potential and saw an opportunity for greatness. His unshakable faith in the sisters, coupled with their own dedication and belief, facilitated the transformation of Venus and Serena into the most successful female tennis athletes the world has ever known. The secret ingredient was Macci's unwavering belief in himself and his prodigious proteges. This magic, which he has shared with countless students including Jennifer Capriati, Andy Roddick, Maria Sharapova, and many more, has changed lives and careers.

"Rewiring a player's mindset to see their playing style and life through a different lens is the cornerstone of connecting mental fitness to physical game-readiness." – Rick Macci

Rick Macci, an icon in the tennis world, passionately advocates for the sport he loves. As a coach, he has held the position of the number one tennis coach in the world for the past century, setting an exemplary standard for all his students. His true gift lies in his ability to address flaws, attitudes, and habits not only in his students' game but also in their thinking. Elevating an aspiring champion's mindset to a profoundly positive state demands concerted focus from both the coach and the student. Throughout his career, Rick has consistently excelled in this aspect, granting him a unique edge as a tennis and life coach. Experts concur that Rick possesses the rare talent to elucidate and present the psychological triggers that significantly impact an athlete's performance.

Earning respect from his industry and the public on a global scale brings immense pride and gratitude to Macci. Over four decades, he has motivated proteges, their families, friends, Hollywood celebrities, and dignitaries, yielding legendary results. His accolades include not just a seven-time USPTA Coach of The Year award and the distinction of being the youngest individual inducted into the USPTA Hall of Fame, but also the remarkable achievements of his students:

- 5 ranked number 1 in the world
- 8 earned Olympic gold medals
- 12 ranked top 10 in the world
- 52 Grand Slam singles titles
- 86 Grand Slam single titles, doubles, and mixed
- 328 USTA Jr. National titles since 1985

Rick's methods are as iconic as his teachings. Rising at 3:00 a.m. daily, he sets a standard of excellence that serves as motivation for everyone, especially his highest-achieving students. His book "Macci Magic" delves into his processes, and his podcast "Game Set Life," hosted with David Meltzer, impacts thousands of players with its positive outlook, work ethic, and honest approach to life and tennis. He's immortalized in the movie "King Richard" for his pivotal role in shaping the remarkable tennis careers of Venus and Serena Williams.

Rick, originally from Greenville, Ohio, continues to work his magic both on the tennis court and on Wall Street. He's an in-demand guest speaker for in-person and virtual events, always captivating his audience with his relatable storytelling about tennis and life. He uses this platform to instruct other coaches on motivating and communicating with their students effectively.

Rick has graced prominent media outlets such as "60 Minutes," the "Today Show," "Good Morning America," "Inside Edition," and more across CBS, NBC, ABC, CNN, USA, ESPN, the Tennis Channel, BBC, Fox News, Fox Business, numerous podcasts, and sports-talk radio shows worldwide.

Connect with Rick Macci on his website at RickMacci.com.

Dr. Nivedita (Niva) Uberoi Jerath hails from Augusta, Georgia, and has been fortunate to receive education and medical training from prestigious institutions including Harvard University for her undergraduate training, Mayo Clinic College of Medicine for her medical training, Harvard University for her neurology training, and the University of Iowa for her neuromuscular and clinical neurophysiology fellowships. She secured a Muscular Dystrophy Association Grant at the University of Iowa to investigate driving ability in patients with CMT1A and received a Masters in Translational Biomedicine.

Devoted to helping her patients, Dr. Niva serves as the Director of Neuromuscular Medicine in Orlando, where her program has garnered national recognition from organizations such as the Muscular Dystrophy Association, ALS Association, Hereditary Neuropathy Foundation, American Association of Electrodiagnostic Medicine, and the Myasthenia Gravis Foundation of America. Driven by a desire to acknowledge her patients with neuromuscular disorders and celebrate their remarkable achievements despite their disabilities, she aims to be an emblem of modern neuromuscular medicine.

Amidst her demanding medical career, Dr. Niva's passion for tennis and mental strength stands out. She emerged as an undefeated junior tennis champion while competing in the Southern Tennis Association. Utilizing mental fortitude, she navigated the arduous years of medical training at esteemed institutions like Harvard, Mayo Clinic, and the University of Iowa, all while excelling in her academic pursuits. Although treating patients who are physically weakened, she recognized the need to support those who are mentally paralyzed and empower them to unlock their full potential.

A prominent figure in her life's journey, Rick Macci recruited her to his academy after she defeated one of his students in a tennis tournament. She holds the highest regard for Macci, describing him as "aMACCIng", a champion of champions, and a wonder of the world. His mentorship guided her path, whether aiming for the pinnacle of her abilities or choosing to attend Harvard University over pursuing a professional athletic career. A robust billion-dollar mindset, fostering intelligent choices have been pivotal in her quest to achieve her dreams.

Follow Dr. Niva on Facebook, LinkedIn, YouTube, Instagram (doctor.niva), or visit her website at https://drniva.com.

REFERENCES

[1] Kahneman, Daniel, 1934- author. Thinking, Fast and Slow. New York :Farrar, Straus and Giroux, 2011.

[2] Maynard, K. (2012). *No excuses: The True Story of a Congenital Amputee Who Became a Champion in Wrestling And in Life*. Simon and Schuster.

[3] Maynard, K. (2012). *No excuses: The True Story of a Congenital Amputee Who Became a Champion in Wrestling And in Life*. Simon and Schuster.

[4] Suganthi. (n.d.). *Slave of my slave*. http://englishclass-diary.blogspot.com/2010/07/slave-of-my-slave.html

[5] Zhou Y, Tse CS. *The Taste of Emotion: Metaphoric Association Between Taste Words and Emotion/Emotion-Laden Words*. Front Psychol. 2020 Jun 5;11:986. doi: 10.3389/fpsyg.2020.00986. PMID: 32581914; PMCID: PMC7290244.

[6] Ketlner, Dacher. (2017). Feeling sad or anxious? Human touch reduces stress and conveys emotion | WIRED UK. https://www.wired.co.uk/article/the-good-life-human-touch

[7] Fields, Dougals R. 2017. When Music Makes You Cry | Psychology Today. https://www.psychologytoday.com/us/blog/the-new-brain/201709/when-music-makes-you-cry

[8] Ferreri L, Mas-Herrero E, Zatorre RJ, Ripollés P, Gomez-Andres A, Alicart H, Olivé G, Marco-Pallarés J, Antonijoan RM, Valle M, Riba J, Rodriguez-Fornells A. *Dopamine modulates the reward experiences elicited by music*. Proc Natl Acad Sci U S A. 2019 Feb 26;116(9):3793-3798. doi: 10.1073/pnas.1811878116. Epub 2019 Jan 22. PMID: 30670642; PMCID: PMC6397525.

[9] Loehr, J. E. L. (1982). *Athletic Excellence: Mental Toughness Training for Sports*. Forum.

[10] Brick, N., McElhinney, M. J., & Metcalfe, R. S. (2017). The effects of facial expression and relaxation cues on movement economy, physiological, and perceptual responses during running. *Psychology of Sport and*

[11] *Exercise, 34*, 20–28. https://doi.org/10.1016/j.psychsport.2017.09.009
[11] Runner's World. (2018, November 2). This is why Kipchoge smiles when he runs (and why you should be doing it too). Runner's World. https://www.runnersworld.com/uk/training/motivation/a776539/how-smiling-improves-your-running/
[12] Migliaccio, G. M., Russo, L., Marić, M., & Padulo, J. (2023). Sports Performance and breathing rate: What is the connection? A Narrative review on breathing strategies. Sports, 11(5), 103. https://doi.org/10.3390/sports11050103. PMID: 37234059; PMCID: PMC10224217.
[13] Blaxton, J. M., Bergeman, C. S., Whitehead, B. R., Braun, M. E., & Payne, J. D. (2017). Relationships among nightly sleep quality, daily stress, and daily affect. *The Journals of Gerontology: Series B*, gbv060. https://doi.org/10.1093/geronb/gbv060. PMID: 26307483; PMCID: PMC5927097
[14] Chen, M., He, Z., Zhang, Z., & Chen, W. (2022). Association of physical activity and positive thinking with global sleep quality. *Scientific Reports, 12*(1). https://doi.org/10.1038/s41598-022-07687-2. PMID: 35256683; PMCID: PMC8901642.
[15] Sharma, A., Madaan, V., & Petty, F. D. (2006). Exercise for mental health. *The Primary Care Companion for CNS Disorders, 8*(2). https://doi.org/10.4088/pcc.v08n0208a. PMID: 16862239; PMCID: PMC1470658
[16] Field, T., Hernandez-Reif, M., Diego, M., Schanberg, S. M., & Kuhn, C. M. (2005). Cortisol Decreases and Serotonin and Dopamine Increase Following Massage Therapy. *International Journal of Neuroscience, 115*(10), 1397 1413. https://doi.org/10.1080/00207450590956459. PMID: 16162447.
[17] Sandberg, S., & Grant, A. (2017). *Option B: Facing Adversity, Building Resilience, and Finding Joy*. Random House.
[18] Mukundananda, S. (2022). *The power of thoughts*. Penguin Random House India Private Limited.
[19] Macci, R. (2013). *Macci Magic: Extracting Greatness from Yourself and Others*. New Chapter Press.
[20] Afremow, J. (2015). *The champion's mind: How Great Athletes Think, Train, and Thrive*. Rodale Books.

[21] BBC News. (2014, January 3). *Natan Sharansky: How chess kept one man sane*. BBC News. https://www.bbc.com/news/magazine-25560162

[22] Jackson, P. L., Lafleur, M. F., Malouin, F., Richards, C. L., & Doyon, J. (2001). Potential role of mental practice using motor imagery in neurologic rehabilitation. *Archives of Physical Medicine and Rehabilitation*, 82(8), 1133–141. https://doi.org/10.1053/apmr.2001.24286. PMID: 11494195.

[23] *Power of Visualization :: Philcicio*. (n.d.). https://www.philcicio.com/power-of-visualization/

[24] Macci, R. (2013). *Macci Magic: Extracting Greatness from Yourself and Others*. New Chapter Press.

[25] Tennis.com. (2021, May 20). *A disability couldn't stop Roger Crawford from excelling on the court*. *Tennis.com*. https://www.tennis.com/news/articles/a-disability-couldn-t-stop-roger-crawford-from-excelling-on-the-court

[26] Canfield, J., & Hansen, M. V. (2012). *Chicken soup for the soul: Stories to Open the Heart and Rekindle the Spirit*. Simon and Schuster.

[27] Whittam, P. (1995). *Tennis talk, psych yourself in to win! Affirmations for Mental Fitness in Tennis*. Saphire Pub.

[28] Macci, R. (2013b). *Macci Magic: Extracting Greatness from Yourself and Others*. New Chapter Press.

[29] Rodenburg, M., & Rodenburg, M. (2021, August 4). *Daily Affirmations Helped Valarie Allman Win Gold. Here's How to Make them Work for You, Too*. Women's Running. https://www.womensrunning.com/events/olympics/valarie-allman-mantras/

[30] Tikkanen, A. (2009, July 24). *Jennifer Capriati | Biography, Titles, & Facts*. Encyclopedia Britannica. https://www.britannica.com/biography/Jennifer-Capriati

[31] *Jennifer Capriati quotes*. (n.d.). BrainyQuote. https://www.brainyquote.com/quotes/jennifer_capriati_26 2023

[32] Clarey, C. (2021). *The Master: The Long and Beautiful Game of Roger Federer*. Twelve.

[33] Macci, R. (2013b). *Macci Magic: Extracting Greatness from Yourself and Others*. New Chapter Press.

[34] Macci, R. (2013c). *Macci Magic: Extracting Greatness from Yourself and*

Others. New Chapter Press

35 *James Lupski's Research into His Disease Paved Way Toward Personalized Medicine | Muscular Dystrophy Association.* (2017, December 12). Muscular Dystrophy Association. https://www.mda.org/quest/article/james-lupskis-research-his-disease-paved-way-toward-personalized-medicine

36 Douglas, G., & Burford, M. (2012b). *Grace, gold & Glory: My Leap of Faith.* Zonderkidz.

37 Douglas, G., & Burford, M. (2012b). *Grace, gold & Glory: My Leap of Faith.* Zonderkidz.

38 Macci, R. M. (2013, p.83). *Macci Magic: Extracting Greatness From Yourself and Others* [Kindle]. New Chapter Press.

39 Murray, S. P. (n.d.). *5 Lessons from Viktor Frankl's book "Man's Search for Meaning" – RealTime Performance.* https://www.realtimeperformance.com/5-lessons-from-viktor-frankls-book-mans-search-for-meaning/

40 Santonastasso, N. (2018). *Victim to Victor: How to Overcome the Victim Mentality to Live the Life You Love.*

41 Santonastasso, N. (2018). *Victim to Victor: How to Overcome the Victim Mentality to Live the Life You Love.*

42 Macci, Rick. Macci Magic: Extracting Greatness From Yourself and Others

43 Emmons, R. A., & McCullough, M. E. (2003). Counting blessings versus burdens: An experimental investigation of gratitude and subjective well-being in daily life. Journal of Personality and Social Psychology, 84(2), 377–389. https://doi.org/10.1037/0022-3514.84.2.377

44 Hamilton, B. (2012). *Soul Surfer: A True Story of Faith, Family and Fighting to Get Back on the Board.* Simon and Schuster.

45 Riedel, S. (2005). Edward Jenner and the history of smallpox and vaccination. *Baylor University Medical Center Proceedings, 18*(1), 21–25. https://doi.org/10.1080/08998280.2005.11928028. PMID: 16200144; PMCID: PMC1200696..

46 Macci, R. (2013c). *Macci Magic: Extracting Greatness from Yourself and Others.* New Chapter Press

47 Smith, S. S. (2013). *J.K. Rowling.* CB Creative Books.

48 Smith, S. S. (2013). *J.K. Rowling.* CB Creative Books.

49 Clear, J. (2020, February 4). *Marginal gains: This coach improved every tiny thing by 1 percent.* James Clear. https://jamesclear.com/marginal-gains

[50] Djokovic, N. (2013). *Serve to win: The 14-Day Gluten-Free Plan for Physical and Mental Excellence*. Zinc Ink

[51] Djokovic, N. (2013). *Serve to win: The 14-Day Gluten-Free Plan for Physical and Mental Excellence*. Zinc Ink

[52] Djokovic, N. (2013). *Serve to win: The 14-Day Gluten-Free Plan for Physical and Mental Excellence*. Zinc Ink

[53] Geoffreys, C. (2015). *Michael Jordan: The Inspiring Story of One of Basketball's Greatest Players: Basketball Biography Books*. CreateSpace Independent Publishing Platform.

[54] Geoffreys, C. (2015). *Michael Jordan: The Inspiring Story of One of Basketball's Greatest Players: Basketball Biography Books*. CreateSpace Independent Publishing Platform.

[55] Macci, R. (2023) Rick Macci Twitter post. https://twitter.com/RickMacci/status/1689179063741521920?ref_src=twsrc%5Etfw

[56] History, H. (2018). *Walt Disney: A Life from Beginning to End (Biographies of Business Leaders)*. CreateSpace Independent Publishing Platform.

[57] Mukundananda, S. (2022c). *The power of thoughts*. Penguin Random House India Private Limited.

[58] Sharapova, M. (2017c). *Unstoppable: My Life So Far*. Penguin UK.

[59] Sharapova, M. (2017c). *Unstoppable: My Life So Far*. Penguin UK.

[60] Williams, S. (2010b). *My life: Queen of the Court*. Pocket Books.

[61] Williams, S. (2010b). *My life: Queen of the Court*. Pocket Books.

[62] Williams, S. (2010b). *My life: Queen of the Court*. Pocket Books.

[63] Williams, S. (2010b). *My life: Queen of the Court*. Pocket Books.

[64] Williams, S. (2010b). *My life: Queen of the Court*. Pocket Books.

[65] Ugandan teen chess queen gaining worldwide notice. (2020, July 6). *The East African*. https://www.theeastafrican.co.ke/tea/magazine/ugandan-teen-chess-queen-gaining-worldwide-notice--1314236

[66] Kom, M. (2013). *Unbreakable*. Harper Collins.

[67] Kom, M. (2013). *Unbreakable*. Harper Collins.

[68] Kom, M. (2013). *Unbreakable*. Harper Collins.

[69] Macci, R. (2013e). *Macci Magic: Extracting Greatness from Yourself and Others*. New Chapter Press.

Made in the USA
Coppell, TX
22 December 2024

43408239R00134